St Cuthbert's Way

from Melrose to Lindisfarne

Ronald Turnbull

Rucksack Readers

St Cuthbert's Way from Melrose to Lindisfarne

Second edition fully revised by Rucksack Readers in 2023 based on the original guidebook by Ronald Turnbull, published in 2010 in a different format.

Rucksack Readers, 6 Old Church Lane, Edinburgh, EH15 3PX

Telephone +44/0 131 661 0262

Email   info@rucsacs.com
Website www.rucsacs.com

Text © Ronald Turnbull 2010, revisions © 2023 Rucksack Readers.

The right of Ronald Turnbull to be identified as the author of this work has been asserted by him in accordance with the Copyright, Designs and Patents Act 1988.

All rights reserved. No part of this publication may be reproduced, stored in a retrieval system, or transmitted in any form or by any means, electronic, mechanical, photocopying, recording or otherwise, without prior permission in writing from the publisher and copyright holders.

British Library cataloguing in publication data: a catalogue record for this book is available from the British Library.

ISBN 978-1-913817-13-8

Designed in Scotland by Ian Clydesdale (ian@clydesdale.scot)

Printed on rainproof, biodegradable paper in the Czech Republic via Akcent Media Ltd of St Neots, UK

The mapping in this book is © Rucksack Readers 2023 and was created specially for this book by Lovell Johns Ltd. It contains Ordnance Survey data © Crown Copyright and database rights 2023 augmented by original field research by the author in 2009 and updated by the publisher 2016-23.

Publisher's note

All information was checked prior to publication. However, changes are inevitable: take local advice and look out for waymarkers and other signage e.g. for diversions. Walkers are advised to check two websites for updates before setting out: www.rucsacs.com/books/scw and www.stcuthbertsway.info

A few parts of the Way are fairly remote, and the weather is unpredictable year-round. In mist or low cloud, competence with map and compass will be useful. You are responsible for your own safety and for ensuring that your clothing, food and equipment are suited to your needs. The publisher accepts no liability for any ill-health, accident or loss arising directly or indirectly from reading this book.

Feedback is welcome and will be rewarded

We are grateful to readers for their comments and suggestions. All feedback will be followed up, and readers whose comments lead to changes will be entitled to claim a free copy of our next edition upon publication. Please send emails to info@rucsacs.com.

Contents

Introduction   4

1 Planning and preparation
- Best time of year and weather   5
- Previous experience   6
- How long will it take?   6
- Accommodation and supplies   8
- Getting there and away   9
- Tides and access to Lindisfarne   11
- Terrain   12
- Altitude profile   12
- Navigation and waymarking   13
- Access, access with dogs   14
- Pronunciation guide   15
- Common Ridings and festivals   15
- What to bring; packing checklist   16

2 Background information
- 2·1 The striding saints   17
- 2·2 History   20
- 2·3 Land and wildlife   22

3 The Way in detail
- Tweedbank to Melrose   28
- Abbotsford House   29
- Melrose   30
- 3·1 Melrose to Harestanes   31
- Jedburgh   38
- 3·2 Harestanes to Kirk Yetholm   40
- 3·3 Kirk Yetholm to Wooler   48
- Wooler   57
- 3·4 Wooler to Fenwick   58
- 3·5 Fenwick to Lindisfarne   64
- Lindisfarne   67

4 Reference
- Useful websites, weather and tides, maps   70
- Access, places of interest, visitor information   70
- Support services, taxis and transport, hostels   71
- Pilgrimage links, Notes for novices and credits   71
- Index   72

Introduction

Study St Cuthbert's Way on the map, and you may expect a slightly tame walk with a tendency to stay at or below the 300 m contour, a selection of Border abbeys, a stretch of the Tweed and a final section apparently underwater.

What the map doesn't prepare you for is the sheer charm of this comparatively short path. Its hills may be small, but they are certainly hilly: from the volcanic knobs of the Eildons clothed in lurid gorse and inhabited by the Queen of Elfland herself to the shapely foothills of the Cheviots, each one cloaked with steep grass and crowned with a hill fort.

Then there are the small woods, some of open pine, some scrubby, some verging on jungle. There are the countless streams, where wild garlic shines among the brown gloom. Even the short road section surprised me: north-east of Wooler a dead rabbit slid along the tarmac, apparently self-propelled, but actually pulled by a considerably smaller stoat.

There's much to enjoy along the Way, but even so, you'll be glad when it's over – glad because you've arrived at Lindisfarne. The 'underwater' section across the mudflats of the Pilgrim Way is unique in British long-distance walking. And the Holy Island of Lindisfarne is one of the country's most magical places.

Many come to St Cuthbert's Way because it is quite short. Many will finish this charming path wishing it were a whole lot longer.

Above Melrose, path onto the Eildons

1 Planning and preparation

From the red stone village of Melrose, the Way heads straight up to 310 m (1020 ft) on the volcanic Eildons. After a half-day along the great River Tweed, it strikes south-east across pastureland and through small woods; first along the line of Roman Dere Street, then climbing gradually through more hilly grassland.

After Morebattle the going gets steeper. You'll climb to 369 m (1210 ft) on Wideopen Hill, and (after crossing the border into England) return to nearly this height across the shapely foothills and heather moors of the Cheviots. From Wooler, lower moorland mixed with arable fields and forestry plantation lead you out to the sea. The final crossing to Lindisfarne is made by road causeway or, more adventurously, barefoot on the ancient Pilgrim Way across 2·5 miles (4 km) of tidal mud and sand.

Through all this variety, the going underfoot is, on the whole, gentle. After the first climb from Melrose, the slopes are neither steep nor unduly long and the Way never ventures above 370 m. Over the 63 miles (101 km), your total ascent is a modest 2250 m (7400 ft): see pages 12-13 for an altitude profile of the whole route. But because many of its paths are grassy, the Way does require some care in navigation compared with more frequented, well-worn footpaths.

The Way is normally walked eastwards from Melrose to Lindisfarne, echoing the progression of St Cuthbert's life: see page 17. On a practical note, prevailing winds are usually from the south-west, so are more likely to be at your back. Moreover, this direction makes the Holy Island of Lindisfarne the fitting culmination of your walk.

Best time of year and weather

The Way can be walked enjoyably at any time between March and October. The wildflowers are at their best in May and June, and the weather tends to be kind. May to July is the nesting season for seabirds of Lindisfarne and the Farne Islands. July and August are holiday months, with Scottish schools breaking for the summer at the start of July. The Way, though never crowded, will be at its busiest in those two months. They also have hazy summer light and some inconvenience from biting insects, so may not be ideal. Autumn colours are at their finest in late October, and autumn brings thousands of wading birds to Lindisfarne.

If you are an experienced walker and don't mind a bit of cold and wet, you could walk the Way in mid-winter. Expect fewer than eight hours of daylight in December, some very muddy paths and a shortage of accommodation. When the sun does come out, winter light over the hills and sea can be magical.

On average, the eastern side of the UK is drier and sunnier than the west. But the weather in Britain is seldom average. Expect at least some sunshine, and also some rain, on your walk. Continuous heavy rain all day long is rare, but not unknown. Low cloud or sea fog (*fret/haar*) can make navigation challenging, so make sure that your route-finding skills are adequate before you set off.

Previous experience

If you've never tackled a long-distance walk before, don't worry: St Cuthbert's Way makes a good choice. The distances between accommodations are not excessive; the terrain mostly has sound surfaces; the gradients are steady with only the odd rough, boggy or steep section; and the waymarking is mostly good, although there are places where you need to stay alert, especially if visibility is poor.

Sound preparation and planning will help you to enjoy the experience to the full. Inexperienced walkers may find it more enjoyable, as well as safer, to have company. Ideally go with somebody whose pace is compatible, or if nervous, attach yourself to an organised group. Book your accommodation well in advance and be realistic in committing yourself to daily distances. In the weeks before, do several all-day walks, if possible on consecutive days, to test your footwear, waterproofs and fitness. Obtain our *Notes for novices* which cover distance planning and choosing walking equipment: see page 71.

How long will it take?

A strong, fit walker in a hurry could snatch the route in a 3-day long weekend – though tidal restrictions at Lindisfarne would probably add a fourth day. But making a proper holiday of it over five or six days allows time to visit at least one of the ruined abbeys, to explore Melrose and Wooler, and to linger on Lindisfarne.

Table 1 presents the distances for a five-day walk. You can add rest days and perhaps split the longer days. If you want to extend the mainland walking over more than five days, you can consider overnighting at any or all of St Boswells, Morebattle and Hethpool. However, you'd be relying on places that have only a single B&B which may be fully booked on the dates that you need, or may have gone over to self-catering by the time you read this. Refer to the facilities table on page 12 for more detail.

Beyond the mainland walk, you must add time for Holy Island itself. You can cross the causeway safely only during two periods in any 24 hours, depending on the tides. The duration of the 'safe periods' varies from just over five hours (at extreme spring tides) to nine (at extreme neaps), so it's worth checking your exact dates ahead of time: see *bit.ly/RR-causeway*. The Pilgrim Way is lower lying so its safe periods are even shorter. But the barefoot approach over the sands and mudflats is a unique experience – well worth researching the tide times and read page 11 carefully.

Rather than hurrying on and off the island on a single tide, it's much better to linger overnight if possible. The tourist tide retreats as the sea advances, making Lindisfarne into a proper island. The sea and the seals approach the shoreline, and evening light plays on the castle walls. However, accommodation on the island is expensive, and camping is not allowed. So some may prefer to spend a daytime high tide on the island, before an overnight at Beal or Fenwick, convenient for a morning bus.

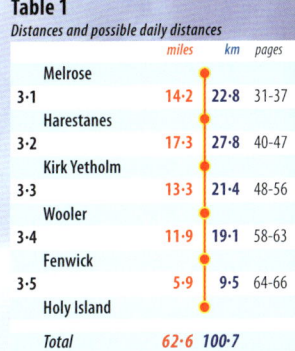

Table 1
Distances and possible daily distances

		miles	km	pages
	Melrose			
3·1		14·2	22·8	31-37
	Harestanes			
3·2		17·3	27·8	40-47
	Kirk Yetholm			
3·3		13·3	21·4	48-56
	Wooler			
3·4		11·9	19·1	58-63
	Fenwick			
3·5		5·9	9·5	64-66
	Holy Island			
	Total	62·6	100·7	

When planning how much time to spend on the Way, remember that you may enjoy some leisure in various places, especially those with ruined abbeys. If you haven't been to Melrose before, you may want to spend a day or half-day there before embarking on the Way: see page 30. At St Boswells, note that to see Dryburgh Abbey you need an extra hour or so for the detour across the river Tweed. You may also want to spend time in Jedburgh to visit its abbey, castle, and royal house. And you may well want to dwell on Lindisfarne for a night or two: see page 67.

You are bound to walk further than the 63 miles in the course of getting to and from the route from your accommodations and evening meals. There are many attractive detours to see abbeys or castles and you may want to climb the odd hill for a better view. Although the Borders Railway gives convenient access from Edinburgh to Tweedbank, that still leaves you with a two-mile walk (or bus ride) to Melrose itself. And given that the centre of Jedburgh is about 3 miles offroute, you will understand why many tour operators arrange a taxi for their walkers from Harestanes which is near mile 14·2. (Options for resuming the route from Jedburgh are discussed on page 39.)

If you walked from Tweedbank to Melrose, you will have covered 16·2 miles (26·1 km) to Harestanes on your first day, which will be enough for many. If that sounds too much for you, you could split the first day at Newtown St Boswells. You could also split other sections: see the previous page. But note that if you taxi back to Harestanes the next day, you face a 17·3-mile walk to Kirk Yetholm, which may be too long for many.

Eildons and River Tweed from Scott's View

Accommodation and supplies

Table 2

	B&B/hotel	hostel	camping	shop	pub/café
Melrose	✓		✓	✓	✓
Newton St Boswells	✓			✓	✓
St Boswells	✓				✓
Jedfoot Bridge/Mounthooly					✓
Harestanes/Monteviot					✓
Jedburgh *(2·5 mi/4 km)*	✓		✓	✓	✓
Morebattle	✓ (orange)			✓	✓ (orange)
Town Yetholm	✓		✓	✓	✓
Kirk Yetholm	✓	✓			✓
Hethpool	✓				
Wooler	✓	✓	✓	✓	✓
East Horton	✓				
Fenwick	✓				✓
Beal *(1·5 mi/2 km)*			✓		✓
Holy Island Village	✓			✓	✓
Beal Road End	✓			✓	✓

Places in italic had only one B&B as of 2023   ✓ Refer to page 44 for the Templehall Hotel

Accommodation along the Way can be sparse, and you need to book in advance at any time of year. Some B&Bs that closed during the Covid pandemic reopened only as self-catering, and others never reopened. All facilities are on or close to the Way unless we show a distance offroute: that is measured from the closest approach to the Way. Table 2 uses italics to distinguish places where in 2023 we knew of only one B&B, often with very limited capacity: a fishing party or small group can fill up an entire village. Bear in mind also that B&B hosts don't normally provide evening meals: if you stay in a rural village you may have a choice between carrying enough food to eat cold as an evening meal, or taking taxis both ways to the nearest town with a pub or restaurant. And some hosts insist on a two-night minimum stay, especially in high season, so consider whether you want a rest day at that location,

The only hostels close to the Way are at Kirk Yetholm and Wooler, open in season. Elsewhere there are country inns and B&Bs which may be quite expensive: in early 2023 £60-£90 per night was a typical *minimum* for a solo walker in each location. Many B&Bs charge virtually the same for a solo walker as for two people sharing – despite the fact that you'll get only one breakfast! Hotels and inns are more likely to have single rooms, so it's worth shopping around. If you are making your own accommodation bookings, be sure to contact the smaller locations first: once those challenges are met, email or phone the places with more choice, such as Melrose and Wooler. Alternatively, use the services of one of the companies that specialise in support services for walkers on this route: see page 71. If you want to bring more stuff with you than you are prepared to carry in your rucksack, you will need their help anyway. Read our packing list on page 16 before deciding.

There are several campsites along the Way. Discreet and responsible wild camping is a legal right in Scotland: see page 13. In England it isn't, not even on the access land defined by the *Countryside and Rights of Way Act*.

The Way remains at fairly low altitude throughout, and there is little if any drinkable water to be found. So refill your water bottle or bladder at every opportunity: most cafés and pubs will oblige a genuine customer. Shops for food supplies are sparse in places. Between St Boswells and Town Yetholm you pass only one shop, the community store at Morebattle: visit morebattlecommunityshop.co.uk to check its opening times. There's no food and drink between Kirk Yetholm and Wooler, nor any between Wooler and Lindisfarne.

Getting there and away

Table 3 shows recommended journey options and times for travel. To reach Melrose from Edinburgh, use the Borders Railway to Tweedbank. Trains normally run twice an hour and take an hour; complete the final couple of miles into Melrose by bus or on foot: see page 28 for directions. You can also reach Melrose from Edinburgh using Borders Buses, but you have to change at Galashiels and it takes two hours or more.

To reach Melrose from Newcastle or anywhere to its south including London, the fastest method is an LNER train from London King's Cross to Berwick upon Tweed, with hourly departures and fast journey times. From Berwick take Borders Buses' number 60 or 67 to Melrose (departures are roughly hourly) or, if time is at a premium, a taxi (37 miles).

Table 3: Distances and journey times to the start and from the finish

from	to	mi	km	means of travel	time (fastest)
Edinburgh (Waverley) *	Melrose	40	63	train to Tweedbank	1hr
Edinburgh bus station *	Melrose	40	63	bus	2hrs
Newcastle upon Tyne *	Melrose via Berwick	100	161	train to Berwick, then bus	2hr 30min
Newcastle upon Tyne *	Melrose	72	116	bus (only 6 per week)	1hr 40min
Berwick-upon-Tweed	Melrose	37	60	bus	1hr 20min
Beal Filling Station ♦	Berwick-upon-Tweed	10	16	bus	21 min
Berwick-upon-Tweed	Edinburgh (Waverley)	57	92	train	41 min
Berwick-upon-Tweed	Newcastle upon Tyne	63	101	train	42 min
Beal Filling Station ♦	Newcastle upon Tyne	59	95	bus	2hrs 6min

* For travel from the nearest airport, add 40–60 minutes to each time: see text
♦ Travel times from Lindisfarne are longer, but vary with the tides: instead we show times from bus stops at Beal Filling Station (TD12 2PD)

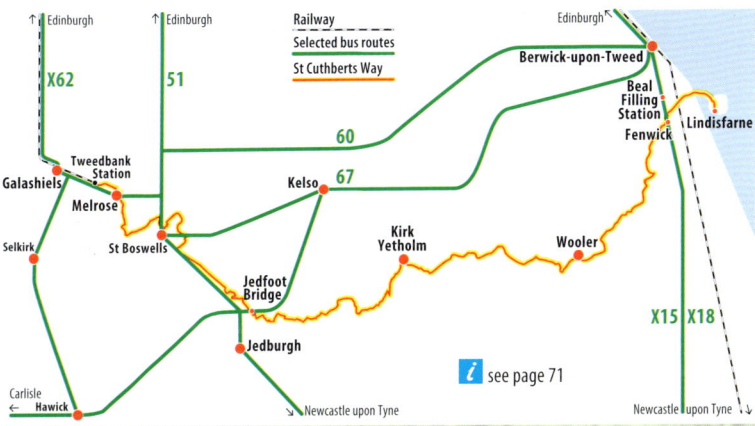

For those travelling by air, Edinburgh has the nearest airport for Melrose. To reach central Edinburgh for onward trains and buses, take the airport bus or tram: both take about 35 minutes to the city centre. From Newcastle airport, trains to central Newcastle are fast (25 minutes) and very frequent. Then you need a train to Berwick and continue to Melrose as above. Should your journey times happen to work with the Peter Hogg 131 (Newcastle to Kelso via Jedburgh), in theory you could take this bus direct from Newcastle airport to Jedburgh, but the 131 departs only 4-6 times per week. Unless starting your walk from Jedburgh, you would still need a Borders Buses 68 from Jedburgh to Melrose (hourly), so in practice a better option is likely to be the train to Berwick upon Tweed, then reach Melrose by bus.

Getting away from Lindisfarne is more challenging: the tides dictate when you can leave the island: see *bit.ly/RR-causeway* for safe crossing times. From Holy Island village, Borders Buses number 477 can reach Berwick in 35 minutes, but it runs only a few times per week, at times that vary with the tides. On some days there will be only a morning bus, on others there's also an afternoon one – but on many days, especially out of season, there are none. Check *bordersbuses.co.uk* ahead of time carefully before relying on this service. Otherwise it makes sense to walk (or take a taxi) back to the mainland, tides permitting, a distance of 5·4 miles (9 km) through Beal to reach Beal Road End (with the Lindisfarne Inn) on the A1 trunk road. From here, Arriva runs buses (X15 or X18) roughly every two hours – northward to Berwick and southward to Newcastle. All Arriva North-east buses stop on request only.

From Berwick, most peoples will use the railway network, but if a bus is more affordable or convenient, there are other options. National Express has an 'express' (non-stop) service but only once daily. In 2023 it left at 17.35 (northbound to Edinburgh, journey time 1 hour 20) and at 12.05 (southbound to London Victoria, journey time 9 hours 30). Megabus has a faster daily coach from Haggerston Castle (1·2 miles north of Beal Road End) southbound to London Victoria, stopping only at Newcastle, Durham, Leeds, Sheffield and Finchley Road. In 2023 it left at 12.45 and took eight hours.

On Holy Island, Lindisfarne Castle is open only in season, and then only when the causeway is passable: for opening dates see *bit.ly/RR-lind-castle*. While the castle is open, there's a frequent shuttle bus from the car park at the north end of the village to the castle. But unless you're footsore or strapped for time, you may well prefer to walk the extra 1 km. And if you are on Lindisfarne out of season, you can still visit the site including Jekyll Garden, Lime Kilns and headland.

Tides and access to Lindisfarne

Holy Island is truly an island for only 3 to 7 hours in every 12. For motorists, there's a causeway which is open when the tide allows. Safe crossing times are found online at *bit.ly/RR-causeway*. They are also posted on a signboard at the causeway's end. The predictions are conservative: we have seen cars crossing up to 50 minutes before the advertised time, so it may be worth turning up earlier. However it would be foolish to try to cross after the last advertised safe time, and strong winds can increase wave height, thus shortening the safe period. If you see water across the causeway, use common sense and turn back – whatever the signboard may say.  The RAF helicopter, coastguard and RNLI are efficient at rescuing stranded people from the causeway or from the raised rescue shelter at its centre. But they do not rescue cars, which are destroyed by immersion in salt water.

If trapped by the tides, phone 999 and ask the emergency operator for 'Coastguard'. Note that rescue is extremely expensive, and the lifeboat is paid for by donations, not by the government. If you have to be rescued, a substantial donation to RNLI is appropriate.

The Way officially crosses by the causeway, which is worth trying to avoid during busy times of day. It's narrow and heavily used, including by coach traffic. It takes about 20 minutes of brisk walking to cover the mile (1·5 km) of road causeway.

The Pilgrim Way is lower lying than the causeway, by up to 2 m/7 ft. The route remains below high tide level for 2·5 miles/4 km, so it's passable for a much shorter period. The advertised 'safe crossing' times refer only to the road causeway. On a falling tide, wait at least an hour after the causeway opens before attempting the Pilgrim Way. And it would be unwise to set out across these sands on a rising tide. Work out when low tide occurs (midway between causeway opening and closing) and set out across the Pilgrim Way before that time.

For example, if the safe period for causeway crossing is shown as 13.00 to 18.00, then low tide is halfway between, at about 15.30. The earliest time for the Pilgrim Way will be about 14.00, and the latest setting-out time would be 15.30. The sodden sand and soft mud makes for slow going: allow at least 90 minutes.

West from Lindisfarne

Terrain

Most parts of the Way boast surfaces that are sound underfoot, often cushioned by grass. However, during and after heavy rain some paths will be boggy or muddy, especially on the descent to Elsdon Burn, so be sure of suitable footwear. There is relatively little road-walking and no great amount of pavement-bashing because it doesn't pass through any large towns.

Most woodland tracks and riverside paths are well-defined and easy to follow, but there are grassy places where the Way is not obvious unless recent footfall has created a path that is visibly trodden. In these areas, learning to spot waymarker posts from a distance is a vital skill, but in low cloud you may have to resort to using map and compass or GPS.

The eastern section of the route is mainly on sound field paths, tracks and minor roads, and many walk to Lindisfarne across the busy road causeway. Preferable for others, however, is the barefoot walk across the tidal mud and sand of the Pilgrim Way, and its soft terrain makes for slow going.

Recurring features that will lower your average speed are stiles. Whilst there are only a couple of ladder stiles left on the Scottish side of the border, they are more common on the English side. A high stile will slow you down much more than a gate, especially if you are carrying a large or heavy pack.

Altitude profile of the Way

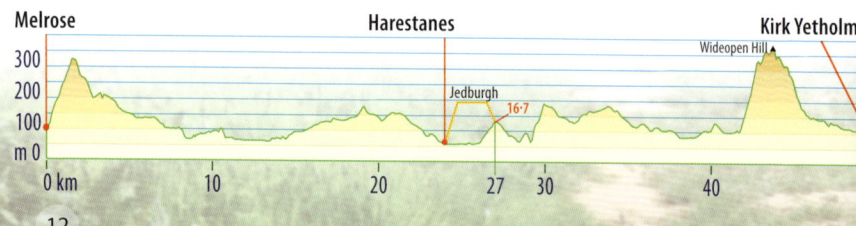

Navigation and waymarking

The Way is waymarked explicitly at almost every turn-off junction, and also at many intermediate junctions. The trail is not heavily used, and where it crosses open field or hill, the path can be narrow and faint in places. Waymarker posts are typically at about 200 m intervals, and they may not always be intervisible if cloud or mist descends.

Be aware of some differences in waymarking between the Scottish part of the route and its English counterpart. In Scotland, the splayed cross symbol is almost always used, often with a directional arrow. On occasion it is combined with another sign, such as the Eildon Hills triple peak or the Roman helmet on Dere Street. Recognise also the Borders Abbeys Way logo which you follow in places, notably if using the BAW link into Jedburgh.

South of the border, signage is more diverse and you need to follow a variety of logos and even on occasion a footpath arrow without any logo; see the top of page 60. Signs that *may* show the Way include the Coast Path curvy N, St Oswald's Way's raven, the National Trail acorn or the words 'England Coast Path'.

Read ahead in the route description and study the map for an idea of where you should be heading. Carry a compass even if you can't take accurate bearings. It will often help you to correct your course without wasting too much time or effort. If relying on your phone for navigation, be sure to carry battery backup, and keep track of where you are on the book's mapping.

This book's mapping shows mileage from Melrose with contour lines at 15 m (50-ft) intervals and a change of colour every 75 m. The scale is 1:40,000 except for pages 28-29 where it is 1:20,000. The grey grid shows km squares and north is always at the top of the page. For more about maps, both printed and online, see page 70 – which also explains how to download our GPX route file.

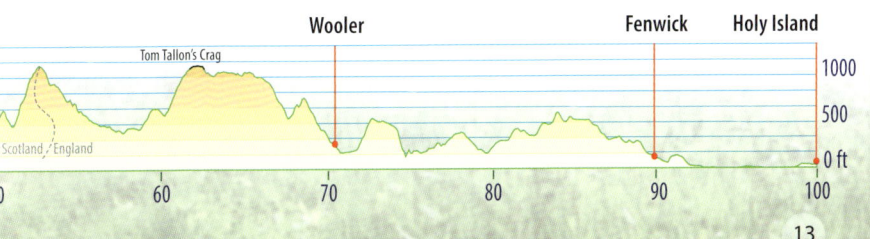

Access

Walkers have free access to the whole of the Way throughout the year and at all times of day. The route straddles Scotland and England, and the access situation on ground beside the path differs in the two countries. In Scotland, walkers have access to almost anywhere provided that access is taken responsibly. Here is the official short summary of rights in Scotland:

Enjoy Scotland's outdoors responsibly

KNOW THE CODE BEFORE YOU GO
outdooraccess-scotland.scot

Everyone has the right to be on most land and inland water providing they act responsibly. Your access rights and responsibilities are explained fully in the Scottish Outdoor Access Code.

Whether you're in the outdoors or managing the outdoors, the key things are to:
- take responsibility for your own actions
- respect the interests of other people
- care for the environment.

Visit **outdooraccess-scotland.scot** for full details. See also page 70.

In England, rights of way are marked on Ordnance Survey Explorers and other maps. In addition, Access Land is marked on recent maps. However, access to so-called Access Land may be withdrawn or conditional. Restrictions on Access Land are given at **www.openaccess.gov.uk**.

Access with dogs

Much of the Way passes through farmland. There may be cattle or sheep alongside the path. So your dog must be under close control, and preferably on a lead. During lambing time, between April and June, your dog will be unwelcome in any fields with sheep. During the same months, birds are nesting on the ground on moorlands, and again dogs must be under very close control. On much moorland in England, dogs are forbidden for all or parts of the year.

Be extra careful near cattle when walking with a dog. The photograph below shows the Way near Hazelrigg, passing between cows and their calves. Approach cattle with caution whether walking with or without a dog. **If cattle react aggressively to your dog, let go of it immediately and take the safest route out of the field.** Useful advice on what the Scottish Outdoor Access Code means for dog owners is in the free leaflet *Dog Owners*: see page 70.

Caution: cows to the left, calves to the right

Pronunciation guide

Most place names in the Borders are pronounced roughly as you would expect, but the table opposite should help with some that might otherwise puzzle.

Common Ridings and festivals

Each year, 11 towns and villages in the Borders celebrate their history with colourful Common Ridings. Some equestrian festivals date back to the troubles of the reiving times; others arose in the aftermath of the Battle of Flodden in 1513. Large numbers of horseback riders re-enact the riding along the historic boundaries ('marches') and the festivals celebrate Borders history, music and song.

Most Riding festivals last for about a week, including including some days of horse ridings. Melrose's Festival Week usually runs for the third full week of June and resumed in 2022 after two years in a virtual format. It runs right after the Borders Book Festival, also held in Melrose. Jedburgh's Riding is known as Jethart Callant's Festival and in 2023 was scheduled from 2-9 July. For details see **www.jethartcallantsfestival.com**.

Wooler hosts the Glendale Festival in July (music and crafts) and also the Glendale Agricultural Show on the August Bank Holiday. For extra atmosphere, time your walk to coincide with the above events. Lovers of peace and quiet may prefer to avoid these dates.

Pronunciation guide

Berwick	berrick
Bowden	bow *rhymes with* cow
Cheviot	cheeviot
Earle	yearl
Eildon	eeldon
Fenwick	fennick
Hownam	hoonam
Teviot	teeviot
Yeavering Bell	yevvering bell
Yetholm	yettum

Fording the Jed Water

What to bring

Those accustomed to hill and moorland walking will already know what they need. The likely contents of a walker's rucksack are shown opposite under 'essential' and should suffice for the Way itself. Some equipment decisions depend on your choice of accommodation and others on whether you use a baggage transfer service: see *bit.ly/scw-support*. Other items (such as midge repellent and sun protection) depend on the time of year.

Carrying a tent and other overnight equipment adds greatly to the overall weight, and also saves money – but then, you'd save even more money by not setting out. Walking the Way should be a pleasure, not an ordeal, and it's more enjoyable without a heavy load. Just pack the essentials for warmth, nourishment and safety.

The Borders is not a wealthy area. Rather than bringing all your needs with you, be ready to spend money along the Way. Using local shops and transport helps to keep them viable for local people as well as for visitors. Post-Covid, contactless and card payments are widely accepted by B&Bs and retail outlets, but it is wise to carry some cash in case of network failure.

Mobile phone (cellphone) reception is fairly good over most parts of the route on most networks. A personal phone is desirable if needing to arrange taxis or lifts into Jedburgh, or if taking the Pilgrim Way: see page 11. A 999 call will be connected via any available network.

Packing checklist

Essential

- rucksack (30 litres minimum)
- waterproof rucksack cover or liner
- walking boots, lightweight if possible
- plenty of specialist walking socks
- breathable under layers
- fleece top layer
- spare clothing for when daywear soaked
- waterproof jacket and overtrousers
- gloves and hat
- compass
- guidebook
- water bottle or bladder (1 litre minimum)
- first aid kit
- credit/debit cards and cash as backup

Desirable

- pole(s)
- mobile phone (cellphone)
- survival bag/space blanket
- whistle and torch
- GPS-enabled device
- gaiters
- slippers/trainers/crocs for overnight
- camera and spares (batteries, cards)
- binoculars (for wildlife)
- notebook and pen
- rucksack pockets/bumbag for small items
- sun cream, sun hat
- midge repellent

Crookedshaws Hill from Wideopen Hill

2·1 The striding saints

During the Dark Ages, starting from various offshore islands, Christianity spread inwards across Britain in small boats and on foot. The Celtic saints were the long-distance walkers of their times. People lived in tribal villages from which it was dangerous to stray into the next glen, but the saints strode from one side of the country to the other – obeying their Master's command to 'take the Gospel to the ends of the Earth'. From St Patrick's settlement at Iona, St Aidan walked diagonally coast to coast to establish his own foundation at Lindisfarne. Aidan was presented with a horse by the Christian King Oswald of Northumbria. As soon as possible, Aidan passed it on to a poor man who, in his opinion, needed it more.

This made sense in practical terms. In unsettled tribal lands, a saint on foot – with no possessions and possibly not even carrying food – would scarcely be worth the trouble of murdering. Also, Aidan just loved long journeys on foot. His successor St Chad was similarly embarrassed by a gift horse, and managed to get rid of it.

Cuthbert, the third Prior of Lindisfarne, was born in AD634 and probably grew up as a shepherd in the Cheviot fringes, or possibly on the Eildons themselves. At the age of 16 he had a vision of St Aidan being carried into Heaven by angels. He embraced the religious life, and became a novice monk at Old Melrose. Within ten years he was its prior. Old Melrose was a few miles east of the present Melrose, in a bend of the Tweed, but almost nothing remains of it today.

Easter tides and the Synod
The Synod of Whitby was held in AD664: see page 18. It settled on the date for Easter as the first Sunday after the first full moon after 20th March. A neat consequence of the Synod is that Easter pilgrims who arrive at Beal Sands on the morning of Good Friday will always find the tide is out, ready for their crossing of the Pilgrim Way.

Statue of St Cuthbert, Lindisfarne Priory

Old Melrose was a substation of Lindisfarne, founded by St Aidan in AD635 and staffed with monks from Iona. A few years later, Cuthbert's abbot, Eata, was appointed Bishop of Lindisfarne, and he took his capable young prior Cuthbert along with him. So St Cuthbert's Way celebrates Cuthbert's life journey from Melrose to Lindisfarne. But for Cuthbert and his colleagues, 62 miles would have been little more than a weekend break. There must have been much monkish walking back and forth between the two foundations, along the old Roman road through the Cheviots and across Glendale.

Cuthbert also walked much further afield. His missionary journeys probably took him to Iona, and he is recorded in Glen Lyon in central Perthshire. Under Hadrian's Wall near Housesteads is Cuddy's Crag, where he probably preached – Cuddy being his Northumbrian nickname. Every year he walked across England to visit his friend St Herbert, who lived on an island in Derwent Water. His colleagues from Lindisfarne are recorded journeying far north into Scotland as well as south to East Anglia and even Tilbury.

At the Synod of Whitby, the crucial church conference of AD664, England adopted the Roman rather than the Celtic version of Christianity and agreed how to set the date for Easter: see the panel on page 17. Cuthbert was there as a conciliator, and in the following years he helped the Celtic style to be absorbed into the Roman one within the Lindisfarne monastery.

In AD676, aged 42, Cuthbert retired early to become a hermit on the Farne Islands. He built himself a small cell, where he prayed and slept. He hacked a well out of bedrock, and scraped together enough soil to grow barley. What stands today as Cuthbert's Chapel dates from about 1300 and was restored in the mid-19th century, using woodwork brought from Durham Cathedral. The stained glass windows show Cuthbert as bishop (left) and hermit (right).

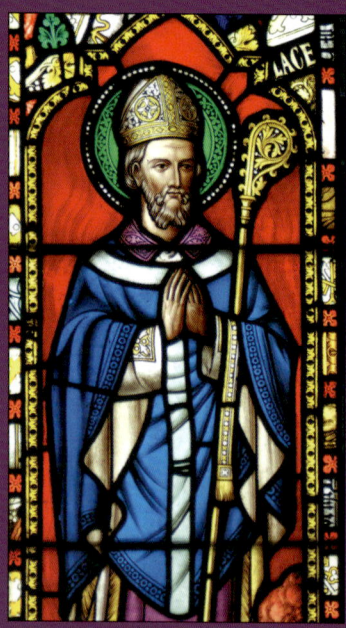

In AD 684, at the age of 50, Cuthbert was summoned back to Lindisfarne to become its bishop. Within three years, his health had broken and he was carried back to his beloved Inner Farne to die. Under his brief, Lindisfarne became the library of the church. Scrolls were inscribed on vellum (specially prepared calfskin). Holy Island had its own vellum factory with two workshops, a slaughterhouse and a midden with the bones of scores of calves. Hundreds of books were hand-written and crafted here.

Immediately after his death in AD687, the famous Lindisfarne Gospels were inscribed in Cuthbert's memory. Their 258 pages consumed 130 calfskins, and involved two man-years of work just for the illustrations. The book's decorations included blue lapis lazuli imported from the foothills of the Himalaya.

In AD698, Cuthbert was dug up and found to be miraculously preserved. In later years, Cuthbert's corpse continued his long-distance travels. Following the first Viking raid on Lindisfarne in AD793, Cuthbert and the Lindisfarne Gospels were carried westwards for safety. On its way to Workington his body rested at Cuthbert's Cave: see page 60.

Meanwhile, the Lindisfarne Gospels en route to Ireland were lost in a shipwreck on the Irish Sea. Cuthbert appeared in a vision and told the monks where to find it again, washed up on the shore. Seawater stains on the gospel, now held at the British Library, corroborate this story.

Later, Cuthbert's corpse reached Ripon, but because of marauding Danes, in AD995 it was moved again to Durham. Here a church was built above his new grave. In 1104 his remains were transferred to a shrine in the newly completed Durham Cathedral. This became a popular place of pilgrimage throughout the Middle Ages.

During the Reformation, Cuthbert's shrine was dismantled but the monks managed to hide his remains. In 1827 Cuthbert's coffin, still containing his bones, was dug up and opened. Around his neck was his beautiful pectoral (chest-worn) cross, made of gold and studded with garnets. His original (AD698) coffin and this cross are on display at Durham Cathedral. A stylised version of the four-armed Cuthbert Cross is used today as the logo of St Cuthbert's Way.

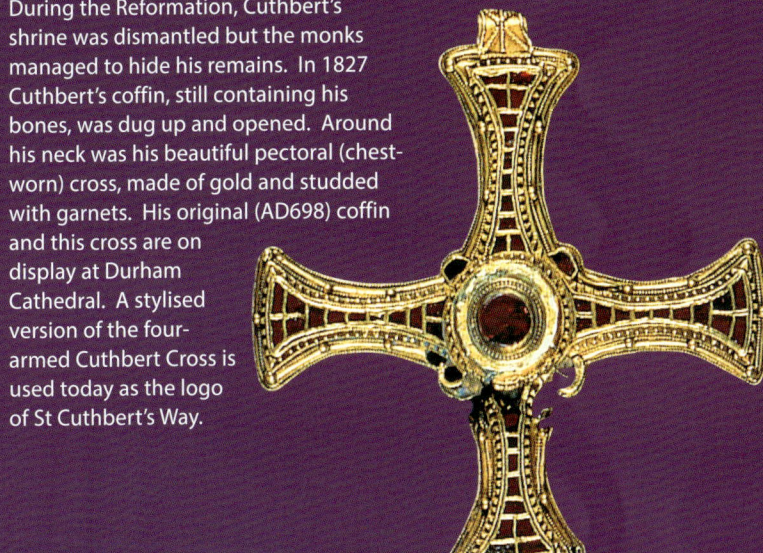

The Cuthbert Cross, Durham Cathedral

2·2 History
Hill forts and Roman roads

Long before St Aidan founded Melrose Abbey, the Eildons were a long-distance path junction. The largest hill fort in Scotland lies beneath the bilberry and heather of Eildon Hill North. This Bronze Age and Iron Age settlement, with its 5km of ramparts, was the capital of the tribe the Romans referred to as the Selgovae.

Roman era grindstone

The steep-sided foothills of the Cheviots provided many more settlements. Covered in short, sheep-cropped grass, these are easier for the non-archeologist to spot. Seven are passed along St Cuthbert's Way, the most spectacular being on Yeavering Bell, where fallen stonework circles the hilltop: see page 52. These Cheviot forts were mainly places of retreat during enemy raids. The one on Eildon was also a permanent settlement, with the remains of 300 hut circles. The huts were of wickerwork and mud, thatched with heather. The people made beautiful pottery, as well as bronze swords and knives. They wore woven woollen cloaks, tunics and hats.

The Romans in turn adopted Eildon as a communications centre. At the foot of the eastern slope they built their large fort of Trimontium, or 'Triple Mountain'. The fort was a large one, with a bath house and an inn for travellers. On Eildon Hill North they built a signal station. Its first use may have been as a survey point for Dere Street, the Roman road across the plains from the south.

In use ever since, Dere Street is the line of several miles of St Cuthbert's Way. Its ruler-like straightness is an obvious clue to its origins, even though no Roman remains are visible on the ground. However, you can see such remains in the museum alongside Melrose Abbey, and also at the Three Hills Roman Heritage Centre in Melrose's Market Square.

As a shepherd, and later as prior of Melrose, Cuthbert was part of a thriving local wool industry. Monks were the entrepreneurs of the Middle Ages, with prosperous abbeys across the Borders: Melrose, Dryburgh, Jedburgh and Kelso.

As the feudal system developed into the nation state, the border abbeys were in the front line between Scotland and its expansionist neighbour England. Melrose Abbey was destroyed and rebuilt several times. Its final destruction was in 1544. Henry VIII wanted to unite the kingdoms under himself by marrying the infant Mary Queen of Scots to his son Prince Edward. In what was called the 'Rough Wooing', he sent the Earl of Hertford to persuade the princess by burning down all four of the border abbeys along with the surrounding countryside.

Fort on Eildon Hill North

The raid culminated in a battle on Ancrum Moor in 1545. The English were outmanoeuvred and defeated. Notable in the battle was a local woman called Lilliard, who took up arms to avenge her lover, killed by the English. Her courage is celebrated in a traditional poem:

The site was supposedly renamed Lilliard's Edge in her honour. However the stump-thumping is derived from the 'Ballad of Chevy Chase', a battle of 150 years earlier. Refer to page 35 for her memorial.

> Upon the English loons
> She laid monie thumps
> An when her legs were cuttit off
> She fought upon her stumps.

['loons' = lads, 'monie' = many]

Reivers and raiders

The Border Wars weren't the worst of it. The two monarchs chose to leave the Borders as a buffer zone between England and Scotland. What was convenient for Edinburgh and London was lethal for those who lived here. For 200 years, no law ran in the Borders but blood-feud and counter-raid. Survival depended on alliance with a powerful local warlord, such as Kerr of Cessford Castle.

The Kerrs (or Kers or Carrs) were a tribe raiding on either side of the border. Come the autumn full moon, a farmer might find the Kerrs (or Elliots, Nixons or Armstrongs) descending, his house burnt, his cattle driven away across the hills, and his family left to starve slowly over the coming winter. The author's own ancestors were once at deadly feud with the Kerrs of Cessford.

With the Union of the crowns of England and Scotland in 1603, law gradually returned to the Borders. The Kerrs became the respectable Earls of Roxburgh. But the legacy of those terrible times remains, and not just in the raucous, horseback 'Common Riding' ceremonies of Jedburgh and other Border towns, nor only in their tradition of seven-a-side Rugby. The scattered population of the Cheviot dales, their eerie silence below the skylarks and the keening wind, can be traced back to the raids and starvation of reiving times.

Dryburgh Abbey

2·3 Land and wildlife

The Way passes through five distinct habitats, described below from west to east:

The Eildons   River Tweed   Farmland   Moor and mountain   Coast

The Eildons

The Eildons stick up almost like volcanoes from their surroundings. Indeed, their rocks were the foundations of volcanoes that erupted here about 300 million years ago. However, their conical shapes are not volcanic, but due to their red trachyte rock being harder and resisting erosion more than the surrounding sandstones. The stonework of Melrose is a mixture of this volcanic rock with the yellowish-brown sandstone of the Tweed valley, giving a pleasing mottled effect.

Stonework of Melrose Abbey museum

The hills themselves are clothed in heather, bilberry, and gorse. This reflects their impoverished, rubbly soil, from which nutrients easily drain away. It also reflects past overgrazing by sheep. Over nearly all of the Southern Uplands, the natural vegetation would be wild woodland of birch and oak. Those trees have been cleared, over centuries, by people and by sheep. Today, upland sheep farming is becoming uneconomic, and these hills are under protection as the Eildon and Leaderfoot National Scenic Area. The natural treeline is moving steadily uphill.

Basalt quarry at the col of the Eildons

Walkers can still enjoy outstanding views from these hilltops, and are likely to spot buzzards soaring in the up-draughts above the steep slopes, mewing like lost kittens. By late summer, a family of half a dozen buzzards may be spiralling in the same upward air current.

Buzzard feeding on rabbit

River Tweed

The Way meets the Tweed at St Boswells. Here it is neither a young river with deeply-carved channel, rock bed and waterfalls; nor a mature river, winding across a wide flood plain. It seems more teen-aged – full-sized and strong, impetuous in its flow. It has in fact 60m still to fall (and 70km of distance to flow) before it reaches the sea at Berwick.

The story of the river is the same as of the land: two centuries of damage by man, now turned around and slowly being restored. The Tweed Foundation has been fencing the banks of the river and its tributaries, allowing tree growth and supporting insects which fall into the river to feed trout and young salmon. The ecology repairs are succeeding. In recent years, the Tweed has been the top salmon river in the entire European Union in terms of the number of fish caught.

The river is home to many ducks, from the common mallard to the rare fish-eating goosander, now breeding here. It is longer and thinner than a mallard, with a saw-tooth beak.

Goosander female (foreground) and male

Herons are abundant, seen at intervals along the river. Other fish predators include mammals such as otter and mink.

Mature salmon work their way up river, reaching the Teviot in late summer, St Boswells a month or so later. After heavy rain with the rivers in spate, they may be spotted leaping up the cauls (artificial weirs) at Melrose, upstream from Mertoun Bridge, and on the Teviot at Monteviot.

Long green fronds and white buttercup-type flowers of water crowfoot stream in the river. On the Tweed's banks at the back of Newtown St Boswells, the rich volcanic basalt soils give a jungle growth of ash trees and rhubarb-like Gunnera. The spectacular giant hogweed also survives here and there along the riverside. Because it causes an allergic skin reaction, it's heavily persecuted by local authorities.

Heron on River Tweed

Water crowfoot below the green footbridge of the Tweed

Oilseed rape below St Cuthbert's Cave

Farmland

Between the Tweed and the Cheviots, the Way passes through pastureland, grazed by cattle and sheep. The rich soils are coloured by the underlying Old Red Sandstone, which formed from sand and silt washed out of an Alp-sized mountain range 400 million years ago. The red debris layered itself across the floor of a shallow sea. At the footbridge of Oxnam Water, the stream has exposed a 20m-high cliff. The sediments built up layer by layer suggest the huge time-span taken to form them. Such sites helped the geologists of the Scottish Enlightenment in the early 19th century to reject the Bible's creation story.

You may well spot brown hare dashing across the pastureland or startle one standing on the road. Other wildlife is found in the field edges, with dog rose lovely in June, and many small birds thriving in the hedges. Woodlands scattered among the fields harbour roe deer, as well as squirrels both grey and red. Throughout the Borders, grey squirrels are inexorably supplanting the native reds.

After Wooler you pass through lower, more fertile farmland, where the rabbit replaces the hare and oilseed rape colours the fields vivid yellow.

Brown hare

Yellowhammer on gorse

Moor and mountain

The foothills on the Scottish side of the Cheviots are small, steep-sided and grassy – just asking to be walked over. And between Morebattle and Wooler, St Cuthbert's Way strides along the 300m contour.

At a wall on Gains Law, the track passes from grassy moorland to heather. The abrupt change at the boundary wall confirms that its cause is land management. Exclusion of hungry sheep has preserved heather moorland – the UK's own special ecosystem. Its notable residents are the red grouse, which depends totally on heather both for food and nest sites, and some heather-adapted caterpillars. In July, the bell heather and cross-leaved heath flower in small clumps on rocky outcrops. A month later, it's the ling, with tiny leaves and flowers, that floats its purple haze across the moorland.

Bedstraw, tormentil and milkwort

By contrast, grass moorland in June offers a tapestry of small bright wild-flowers: white bedstraw, yellow tormentil, and tiny blue flowers of milkwort. Overhead, the sky is full of the sound of skylarks. A small brown bird with two white flashes in the tail is the meadow pipit. The wheatear is another small brown bird, but with a single white flash on its rump – its name derives from 'white-arse'.

Heather moorland, home to red grouse (inset)

Oystercatcher

Coast

The coastal end of the walk is its climax. Here is a very different sort of scenery, symbolised by the crabs met on the 4 km Pilgrim Way crossing. The mudflats, salt marshes, and dunes of Holy Island are a national nature reserve, which naturalists will want to study in advance. Fragments of fossil sea-lilies (crinoids) found on the foreshore are known as St Cuthbert's beads.

Most walkers will miss the winter waterfowl, which include Brent goose, widgeon, and bar-tailed godwit. Walkers who cross and return during a single low tide will only glimpse the oystercatchers, terns, and seals – both common and grey. For good sightings of all these, as well as gannets, puffins, and eider duck, stop over and experience the place as a true island, with the sea lapping at its shoreline.

St Cuthbert's Way is completed here. But a tempting postscript is the boat trip from Seahouses to the offshore Farne Islands. The islands are the absolute end-point of the Great Whin Sill (the volcanic rock which crosses northern England). From May to July there is an amazing display of seabirds, nesting just beside the designated pathway. Moreover, it was Cuthbert's chosen final resting place. On the Farne Islands he built his hermitage retreat, surrounded by sea-spray and the haunting cry of the 'Cuddy Duck', the eider duck whose Northumberland nickname recalls the saint himself.

Eider duck

Tweedbank to Melrose

From Tweedbank station, Melrose High Street is a 10-minute bus ride away: Borders Bus operate numbers 67 or 68 about twice an hour. Rather than wait, consider the alternative of starting your walk with this pleasant 2-mile (3·2 km) riverside route to Melrose.

- Beyond the station, go straight ahead along the 'Melrose Link' cycleway with a blue sign 'Melrose 1¾ miles'. After 500 m, cross a minor road and bear left at the green Southern Upland Way sign to descend to the B6374.

- Cross to its far side, where a timber fingerpost points right, through a timber gate. Head downhill on the narrow path, muddy in places, past an information board for Skirmish Hill (1526). Descend to the lovely river bank: see pages 24-5 for more about the Tweed.

- Continue downstream on an undulating path, briefly leaving the bank at a timber waymarker (thistle in hexagon) to pass through a kissing-gate. The route joins a road fleetingly, then descends a flight of steps near the Chain Bridge.

- After 1 mile (1·6 km) of path, descend steps to the riverside and look for the fingerpost where the SU Way continues ahead. Instead, turn right, signed for Melrose town centre with a blue E2 sign.

- Bear right on the tarmac path between Melrose Parish Church and the war memorial to reach a crossroads. Turn left along the High Street past the Greenyards (rugby) to reach the town centre. The route continues on page 31.

Abbotsford House

Abbotsford House was built by the writer Sir Walter Scott (1771-1832) as a family home, and to display his valuable collection of books, artefacts and weaponry. His Waverley books were, for nearly a century, Europe's most popular novels. His study and library still have his writing desk and books exactly as he worked from them. Reopened in 2013 after major refurbishment, the house and gardens welcome visitors daily from March to November. The visitor centre (admission free) and restaurant are open year-round: see **www.scottsabbotsford.com**. Abbotsford is about a mile from Tweedbank station, served by bus. We recommend the riverside route from Tweedbank station shown on the map clip (1·3 miles/2·1 km), although you could save 450 m by cutting the corner and sticking to the streets.

Bust of Walter Scott, Abbotsford House (library)

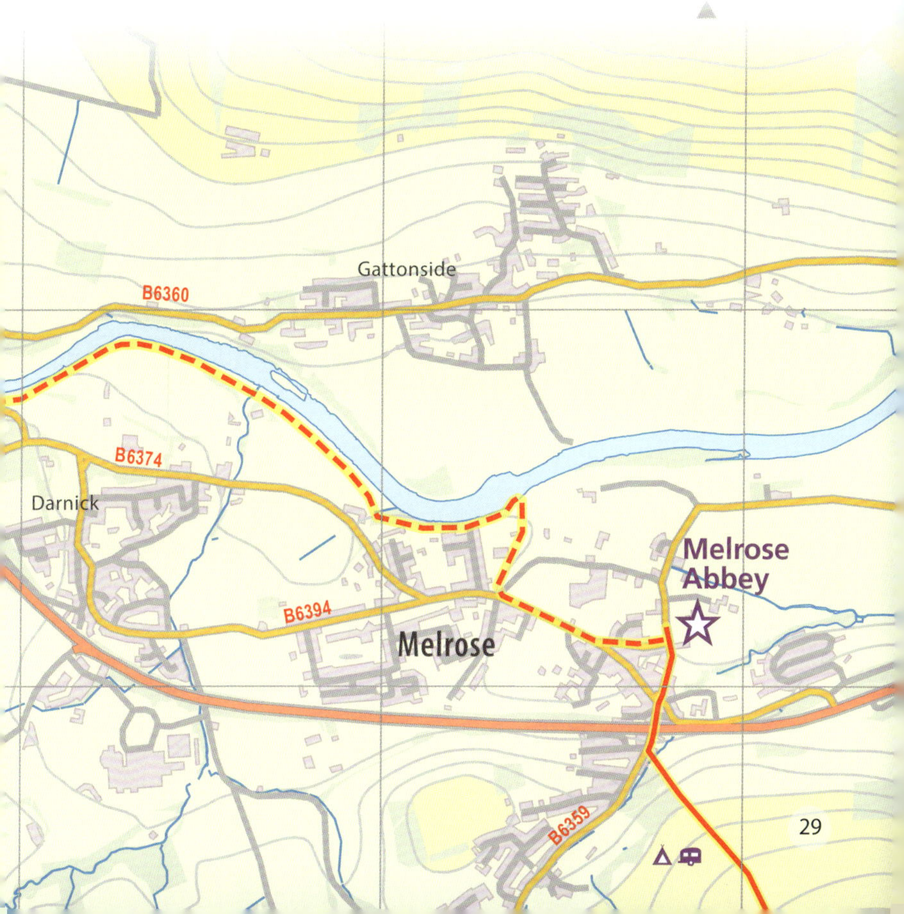

Melrose

The Way starts at Melrose, where St Cuthbert himself started his religious life, becoming its prior around AD660: see page 17. Melrose Abbey was destroyed by Edward II in 1322, and rebuilt by King Robert the Bruce, whose embalmed heart is buried beside the abbey. In 1385 the abbey was burned again by Richard II. The final destruction was in the 'Rough Wooing' of 1544: see page 21.

Marker for Robert the Bruce's buried heart

Melrose Abbey (below) can be appreciated from the surrounding streets, and in early 2023 the abbey itself was closed while masonry inspection was under way. Once it's open again, it's well worth the small entry charge to enjoy its interior, ascend the staircase to the viewpoint on top of its walls, and visit its small museum. The abbey is normally open daily year-round, with earlier closing from October to March – visit www.historicenvironment.scot and search for Melrose.

After the Middle Ages, the focus of Melrose shifted from religion to commerce. The cross that once stood at the entrance to the Abbey precinct also shifted and became the town's Mercat Cross. Almost all of the original cross has been replaced: the oldest part we see is its octagonal base, built only 150 years ago. The rest dates from various times in the last century – with one exception, the metal staple. Petty criminals were tethered to the cross by an iron neck-chain (called the jougs) attached to this staple.

The Roman Heritage Museum is also in the town's Mercat Square. In 2023 it was open Tuesday to Saturday from February and daily from April to October: see www.trimontium.co.uk.

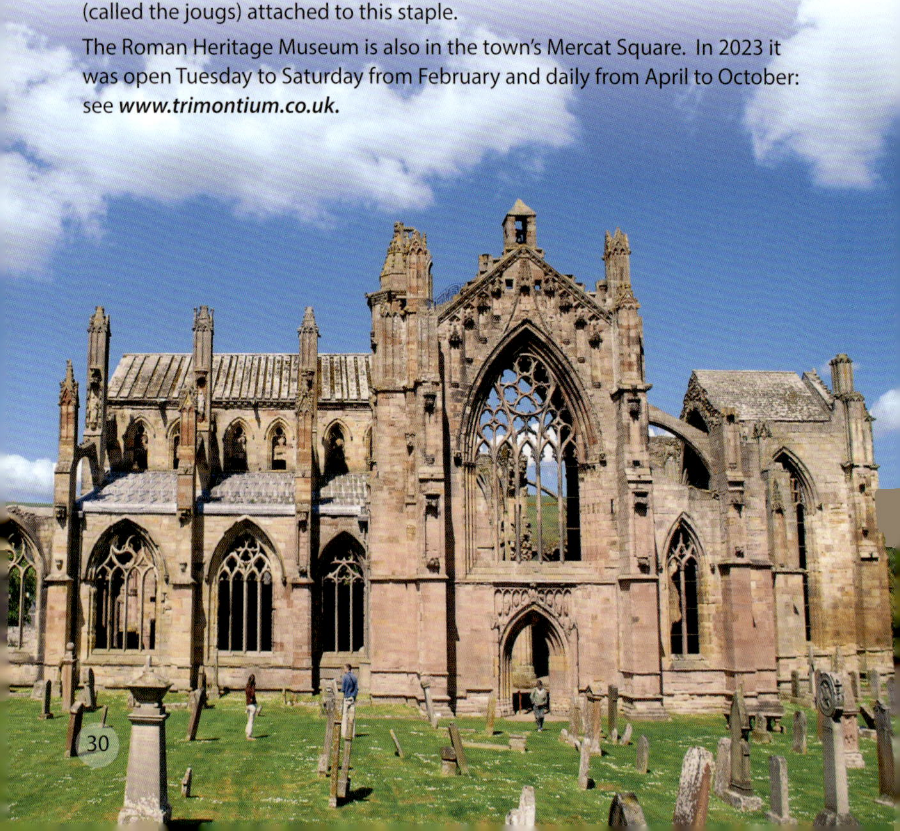

3·1 Melrose to Harestanes

Distance	14·2 miles 22·8 km	
Terrain	paths, sometimes muddy or steep, and woodland tracks, with a couple of short sections on quiet roads	
Grade	starts with stiff climb to 310 m in the Eildons, then more gradual descent followed by undulations beside the Tweed and on the Roman road	
Food and drink	Melrose (wide choice), Newtown St Boswells (café, Dryburgh Arms, shops), Woodside Gardens (café), Harestanes (café), Jedburgh (wide choice but off route)	
Summary	the steepest ascent of the entire Way, rewarded by fantastic views; afterwards easy going on the Tweed bank and along field edges, following the line of Dere Street to end at Harestanes	

33 35 37

0·0 — 4·6 — 4·8 — 4·8 — 14·2
Melrose — 7·4 — Newton St Boswells — 7·7 — Maxton — 7·7 — Harestanes

- From the High Street, bear left along Buccleuch Street to meet Abbey Street: turn left to detour to the entrance to Melrose Abbey.

- From the abbey entrance, head south up Abbey Street, past the high wall of Priorwood Garden on your left. Go straight across Market Square into Dingleton Road, following signs for St Cuthbert Way and Eildon Walk.

- Pass up under the bypass, and after 100 m turn off left down steps. A path heads up 133 wooden steps in a wood, then uphill between fields, through gates and onto open hillside.

- Bear right, still climbing, to go around Eildon North, and up to the col between Eildon North and Eildon Mid Hill at mile 1·2. Look behind for fine views over Melrose, and ahead for wide vistas to the south. For even better views, consider a detour up Eildon Hill North on your left: see the panel.

> **Eildon Hills**
>
> We suggest a detour to the summit of Eildon Hill North for a good path to an airy viewpoint over the broad valley of the Tweed towards the Southern Uplands (to north and west) and the Cheviots (in the south).
>
> From the col, various wide paths rise to the summit plateau. The earthworks and Roman signal station are hidden under the heather and bilberry, but in low sunlight you could make out the large encampment on its southern flank. Return by the same path to the col to resume the Way..

- Head down between the hills on a path among gorse and heather into woods. soon reaching a track junction. Bear right, briefly on the level, then gently downhill.

Eildon Mid Hill from Eildon Hill North

- The track starts to bend uphill, but the Way forks left on an informal path that runs downhill just inside the wood, partly fringed by beech hedge.
- At the wood's bottom edge (mile 1·9), turn right on a path that runs parallel to a lane visible to your left, below. After 400 m at a path junction, turn left to cross the lane and go into a stand of Scots pines.
- The path heads up steps under the pines for 100 m. It continues gently downhill, to reach Bowden's main street at the village's Pant Well (drinking fountain). Built in 1861, it was restored in 2012 : see its interpretation building on the left.
- With signs for Bowden Kirk, turn right along the B6398 and left after 60 m onto a minor road. After 220 m, this road bends right: instead turn left along a narrow, stony path.
- The path runs down to cross Bowden Burn by a footbridge before heading up right to join a track. This continues downstream and above the burn, to a road corner at Whitelee.
- Keep ahead along this road past Whitelee. At mile 4·5 the road goes under an old railway and over a stream, to reach the B6398 which is Newtown St Boswells' main road. To detour to the village, which has the Dryburgh Arms, shops, café and bus stop, turn left here.
- The Way crosses the main road diagonally right into a tarmac lane that dips then rises to a red stone building. Turn left into a lane with a green sign which also serves the Borders Abbeys Way. The lane twists down towards the A68 flyover.

Pant Well, Bowden

Bowden from the south

- Just before the flyover, look for a signed path that forks right into scrubby woodland, soon crossing a footbridge over the Bowden Burn. Keep ahead through the woods, then continue up a total of 56 steps (over three flights) to a high river bank.
- The path heads downstream by the Tweed, later with a viewpoint bench offering views of river, Eildons and a green suspension bridge. At mile 5·3 descend to cross a lane – unless you want to divert to Dryburgh Abbey across the green bridge: see panel.

Dryburgh Abbey
Peaceful among its trees, Dryburgh Abbey has a special atmosphere. It's invisible from the south bank, and to visit it you must cross the Tweed by suspension bridge (and pay an entry charge). Across the river, follow the lane downstream to a junction. Keep ahead to the car park at the Abbey entrance. It's open daily: for hours, see www.historicenvironment.scot. To return to the Way, either retrace your steps, or follow the Borders Abbeys Way (north of the Tweed) as far as Mertoun Bridge, and cross it to rejoin the Way: see map.

- Keep ahead on a track for 100 m, then bear right on a path that remains close to the Tweed, with steps and railings in many places. After a footbridge at mile 6·1 the path bends up right to a road at the edge of St Boswells, where you turn left along Hamilton Place to the village green.

Mertoun Bridge

- Turn left at the green, keeping ahead on the B6404 Main Street to pass shops including Mainstreet Trading, a bookshop with a great café and deli. After 400 m turn left up Braeheads Road.
- Follow the street uphill around to the right, and at its far end turn left down the access road to St Boswells Golf Club. After 220 m look for a path that turns off to the right. This runs beside the golf course and after about half a mile reaches the banks of the River Tweed.
- The path follows the river, at mile 7·8 climbing steps to cross the B6404 road at Mertoun Bridge (built in 1841). Beyond it, descend to resume the river banks: notice, and avoid contributing to, their erosion.
- After a further half mile it passes below Crystal Well, an antique water-pumping station for Benrig House above. Detour to the right up the grassy ramp for a plaque about 'Every Modern Convenience' in this extrordinary house.
- The path now bears right up 62 steps and continues along the bank top overlooking the Tweed. Then it descends by more steps into a wood with wild garlic. After crossing a track and then a footbridge, the path climbs by more steps and a ramp.
- The path passes the historic Maxton Kirk, dedicated to St Cuthbert and mainly dating from the mid-18th century, albeit its bell was cast in 1609. Reach a lane and follow it around to the right for 300 m to the A699 road at Maxton.

Tweed opposite St Boswells golf course

- Turn right along the road for 180 m, then left into a lane signposted 'Longnewton'. The lane crosses an old railway then bends right. About 350 m after the bend, note the tarmac lane at the Morridgehall sign at mile 9·9 ❶. We recommend this unofficial option, as long as you exercise your access rights responsibly: see page 14.

Turn left on the lane that after 350 m bends right and passes Old Morridgehall Farm and newer buildings. The tarmac soon gives out and you continue up a rough track through former woodland. After 800 m, this rejoins the main Way at mile 10·6. Turn left along a track along the line of Dere Street, the old Roman road, and skip the next two bullets.

- Meanwhile the official Way sticks to the lane until just before the busy A68, where it turns left on an earth path under trees near the main road.
- The Way runs along the right-hand edge of a field, then again in trees, to reach a grass track along Dere Street, waymarked with a Roman helmet logo. This becomes a field-edge path that runs straight for the next 5 km.
- At the top of a climb through woodland, at mile 11·8 a stile on the right leads to the wall-enclosed Lilliard's Stone: Stone: see photo below and page 21.

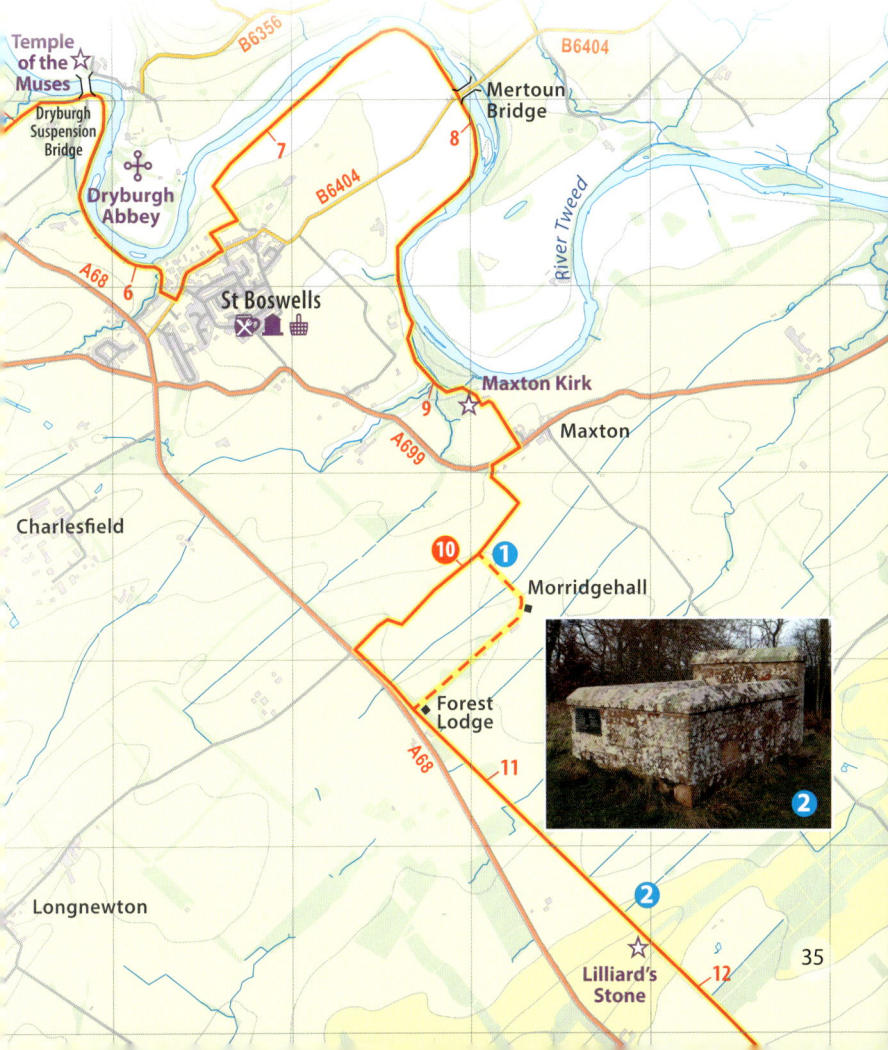

- At mile 13·3 the path reaches a lane: cross over and continue ahead.
- After 750 m, the path crosses a stream and then turns slightly right. After the next footbridge, you could detour up a signed path on the right which leads within 100 m to Woodside Plant Centre with Tearoom.
- Otherwise, at the next lane cross to a small gate. Keep ahead across a footbridge where the Way turns left at a signpost. To continue the Way, skip to page 40. To reach Harestanes, instead turn right and follow this wide path for 150 m. Look out for multicoloured waymarks and a small path that forks down to the right. It joins a tarmac lane leading to Harestanes (café usually open 10.00-16.00: *out-thereartisan.co.uk*) – a recognised rendez-vous for lifts and taxis.
- If you are walking on to Jedfoot Bridge on the A698, it's a further 2 miles/3.2 km along the Way from here. Then there's a further 2.6 miles/4.2 km to central Jedburgh via a lane running east of Jed Water. So this is a good moment to ensure that you have enough energy and daylight to complete a further 4.6 miles/7.4 km.
- Once you've picked up the lane (see the top of page 41), navigation is easy: follow it for 1·9 miles (3 km) to reach the A68, then cross over and follow 'Borders Abbeys Way' waymarks along the Waterside Walk (upstream on the Jed Water's east bank).
- Keep ahead on back streets, then cross an old road bridge over the Jed Water. Bend around left to join the High Street to Jedburgh Abbey, and find your way to wherever you are staying.

Victorian jubilee fountain, Jedburgh

Jedburgh

Jedburgh (formerly Jethart) has much to offer the visitor. There's the 12th-century Augustinian Abbey, still impressive in ruins. Mary Queen of Scots' House is a handsome stone building, formerly thatched, containing furnishings, tapestry and armour from the 16th century. Mary fell dangerously ill with a fever here in 1566. Later, during her long captivity in England, she wished: 'Would that I had died in Jedburgh'.

At the south end of the town you can sample Victorian prison life at the Castle Jail. Throughout the handsome town centre you can enjoy its free wifi and perhaps buy Jethart Snails – a brown boiled sweet supposedly introduced to the town by prisoners from Napoleon's army.

Only 10 miles from the English Border, in the lawless Scottish Middle March, Jedburgh was at the heart of the raids and skirmishes of the reiving times. The town held its own among the local warlords, forming an alliance with Kerr of Cessford (see page 44) against the rival Kerrs of Ferniehurst. For many years, indeed, the town and the Kerrs of Ferniehurst were formally at feud.

During one local war in 1572 a messenger arrived at the town with messages from Mary Queen of Scots. The town was loyal to her infant son, King James VI, and made the messenger eat his own message. The town had its own, much-feared, battle cry: 'Jethart's here!'. Jethart justice consisted of hanging a man first and trying him afterwards: the Jethart staff was a long-handled battle-axe for use on horseback. Its coat of arms bears the motto *strenue et prospere* (earnestly and successfully).

The town's robust heritage lingers on in the Jethart Hand Ba', a version of medieval football played every February with half the town in each team, based around the Mercat Cross. Its leading event is the Callant's Festival, the town's Common Riding: see page 15.

Jedburgh Abbey

Decide how to resume the walk the next day. If you took a taxi from Harestanes, you may have arranged to taxi back and resume the Way from there: refer to page 40. If you walked from Jedfoot Bridge you may wish to return to it and resume from page 41. However, if you don't mind missing a small section of the Way (only 0.6 miles/1 km from Jedfoot Bridge), you may prefer to rejoin the Way at mile 16·7 using the Borders Abbeys Way link. This short-cut is described below and shown on map page 37.

- Start by retracing your steps along Waterside Walk, cross the A68, and go back up Woodend (the small lane). Look out for waymarkers for the Borders Abbeys Way, which you follow for the next 1·5 miles.
- After the lane's first steep climb under trees, ignore the first road on the right, but 250 m afterwards, fork right on a lane past houses and farm buildings. It rises to pass a comms mast at its highest point, then descends slightly. Enjoy great views of Peniel Heugh with its monument to the north: see below.
- Where the lane bends right at a house, turn left to a field path. Beyond the house, join a hedged path to the T-junction with Dere Street where you rejoin St Cuthbert's Way: turn right uphill and follow directions from page 41 bullet 2.

Waterloo Monument from Mount Ulston path

Waterloo Monument
The Tweed valley is dotted with small hills that proved inviting to builders of monuments and follies. Most prominent of these is the 150 ft-high Waterloo Monument on Peniel Heugh. The first attempt at a monument, a massive stone pyramid, stood for less than a year before collapsing 'with a tremendous crash'. Its replacement, a column with spiral staircase, was completed in 1824.

3·2 Harestanes to Kirk Yetholm   42 43 47

Distance 17·3 miles (27·8 km)
Terrain paths through fields and woods, followed by grassy paths over modest hills
Grade undulates for the first 11 miles then climbs to a summit of 369 m (1210 ft) on Wideopen Hill, with a steepish descent to the valley of Bowmont Water
Food and drink Jedburgh (wide choice but off route), Morebattle (shop, hotel), Town Yetholm (shops, hotels), Kirk Yetholm (hotel)
Summary once across the Teviot, the Way rises to high pastures alternating with small woods for the first half; after Morebattle, climb grassy Wideopen Hill

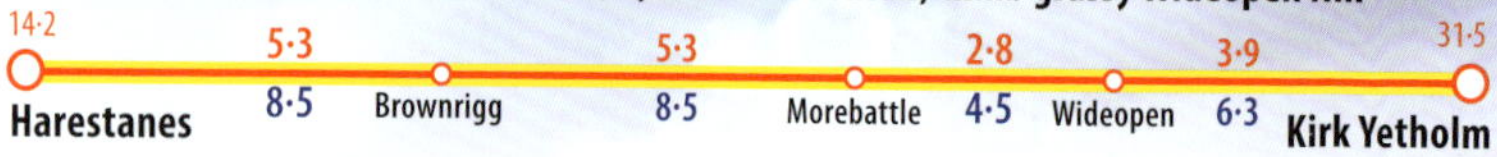

14·2	5·3		5·3		2·8		3·9	31·5
Harestanes	8·5	Brownrigg	8·5	Morebattle	4·5	Wideopen	6·3	Kirk Yetholm

- From the footbridge near Harestanes, the main Way turns left at a signpost (see page 36 bullet 3) and goes through the woods. You emerge to cross the driveway of Monteviot House: if you're here on a summer afternoon you might wish to consider a detour to visit its gardens: see panel.

- The Way goes left along the driveway briefly, but within 60 m turns right through the woods beyond. The woodland path swings right and emerges into a field, where it heads directly downhill into trees beside River Teviot.

- The path bends right upstream for 400 m to a suspension bridge at mile 15·1. Cross the Teviot and turn left, down-stream. At mile 15·7 the path bends right and follows the Jed Water upstream for 450 m before ascending to a crash barrier beside Jedfoot Bridge.

Monteviot House and gardens

Monteviot House is home to Lord Lothian, a descendent of the Kerr cattle-reiving family. The elegant sandstone house is Georgian, with later additions. Its 'eccentric and tangled' interior has fine plaster ceilings and family portraits. The house is open to the public only in July 1200-17.00 (not Mondays).

Superbly located within a curve of the River Teviot, the gardens are open daily 12.00 to 17.00, April to October. A laburnum tunnel leads to a water garden created from a spring-fed bog. House and gardens charge for entry (in 2023 £6 each): www.monteviot.com.

Monteviot gardens

- Turn left beside the A698 for just 70 m to cross the Jed Water, then cross the busy road with great care to go up a lane. (Alternatively, if in need of refreshment, don't cross but continue 350 m to the east for the Caddy Mann: in 2023 it was open 10.00 to 16.00 but closed on Mondays and Tuesdays.)
- After 100 m the Way forks left uphill on a stony track (Dere Street) whilst the lane continues for 1·8 miles (2·9 km) into Jedburgh. (If Jedburgh is your goal, consider sticking to the Way as far as the fingerpost at mile 16·7 to reach it by a pleasanter route, mainly offroad: see map page 37.)
- The Way continues uphill on Dere Street for a further 200 m beyond the fingerpost. Turn left at a horse stile into a patch of woodland, and follow the narrow green path for nearly a mile (1·5 km) to a lane.

Dere Street south-east of Jedfoot Bridge

- Turn right for 300 m to where the lane bends right. Here bear left onto a broad track leading down to Oxnam Water, which you cross by a footbridge on the left at mile 18·2 ❶. Just upstream is a fine outcrop of Old Red Sandstone: see the dark stone near the centre of the photo below.
- After the footbridge, turn left and cross the riverside field diagonally, up to a fingerpost at a gate. As the slope eases a bit, turn left (as signed) to approach trees, then turn right up to a gate near a house (Littledeanlees Cottage). A line of telegraph poles march up this field marking your goal at the top near the cottage.
- The Way now passes around three sides of a rectangle to bypass both house and stone building to its south. It is clearly signed and channel-fenced in places. Once you reach its access road, you are heading east again: climb steeply uphill for 400 m and turn left into woodland at mile 18·7.

North-west over the footbridge across Oxnam Water

- The path heads north under tall beeches to reach another lane. Turn right for 400 m to a T-junction. Make a dogleg by turning left along the road for 40 m, then right through a kissing-gate just before Brownrigg, an eclectic mixture of vernacular stone and modern houses.
- Head down to cross a footbridge, then skirt around the foot of a field. This leaves you heading uphill (east) on a waymarked track into some trees at mile 19·9. This is the first of three woodlands in this section.
- Bear left to follow the track down into a dip. As it rises again, it narrows to a path which runs along the left edge of the woodland to a gate at its corner.
- The path continues along the edge of a field, then the right edge of the second wood, which is of Scots pines. Keep straight on along the right edge of another field, and turn left at its corner.

- Turn right over a wall stile to head slightly uphill with a wall on your right, to the third wood – a hilltop plantation of Scots pines at mile 21.
- Turn left beside the wood and right around its corner to pass along its northern edge. After 400 m turn left away from the wood at a junction.
- The track now runs downhill all the way to Cessford at mile 22·1. Bear right over a stream to Cessford Farm, where you turn left. The road leads towards and past Cessford Castle: keep ahead to the next gate (mile 22·4) for a closer look at its exterior.

Cessford Castle

Interpretation boards present the uncertain and uncomfortable life of the fortress in the reiving times. Cessford was the stronghold of a branch of the Kerr family – equally feared on both sides of the border. Robert Kerr of Cessford was the most notorious raider, blackmailer and feuder of the late 16th century.

According to legend, many of the Kerrs were left-handed. While most refuge towers had a spiral staircase that ran clockwise to favour the right arm of swordsmen retreating upwards, the Kerr strongholds had their staircases spiralling the other way. Sadly the stonework is too dangerous to verify this.

Cessford Castle

- After the castle, descend all the way past the entrance to Otterburn House and its boundary wall to reach the B6401 at mile 23·8. Turn right into Morebattle. Morebattle's name has nothing to do with fighting, but means 'marsh settlement' – from Linton Loch, the swamp that once lay just to its north. Its community shop is open daily: see **morebattlecommunityshop.co.uk** for more. There is, or may be, the Templehall Hotel at the far end of the village but as of early 2023 its opening hours were very restricted and its future uncertain: visit **www.templehallhotel.com** to check on opening hours and what is on offer.
- At the far end of Morebattle, bear right up a lane signed Hownam. At mile 25·6 it drops to meet a road, where you turn right.
- Follow the road beside the Kale Water and within 600 m, just after a ford, turn left to cross it by a footbridge. Cross a field to join a track and turn right on it.
- The track passes up to the right of an old quarry, then zigzags uphill to a point behind a small hill fort. Turn right through a gate and head uphill to the right of a plantation at mile 26·5.
- The path heads uphill through gates to pass just left of the first hump, Grubbit Law (326 m), at mile 26·8. There are fine views north to the Eildons in this section. Bend left to join a stone wall and follow its southern side.
- Head along the main ridge line keeping the wall on your left until you cross it by a ladder stile on the second summit hump.

West over the plantation at mile 26·5

View from Wideopen Hill

- The path and wall continue to the third summit, Wideopen Hill. At 369 m (1210 ft) this is the highest point of the Way, but don't be misled by the plaque that claims it also as its halfway point: this is on the Yetholms bridge see page 46.
- Follw the ridge wall to the right, downhill, before it bends back left. Continue the descent on a spur of Crookedshaws Hill, always keeping close to the wall and crossing it only by a waymarked ladder-stile. In mist, maintain your direction as NNE (022.5°).
- Enjoy fine views to your right over the valley of the Bowmont Water. As the descending ridge reaches fields, the path turns right through a gate in a wall (photo below): below to the right, note a clump of trees. After the gate, descend on a broad path through bracken to a walker gate beside a field gate.

Wideopen Hill

Rising steeply at the northern edge of the Cheviots, Wideopen offers great views over the plains of the Tweed. In the west is the Waterloo Monument, with the triple top of Eildon beyond, 16 miles away as the crow flies. Below you, in the same direction, low sunlight may reveal the Iron Age settlement on Morebattle Hill.

North-east, the ridge points along Bowmont Water to Kirk Yetholm. Behind Yetholm Law gleams the water of Yetholm Loch. To the south the views are shorter, rising to the ridgeline of the Cheviots with the English border along the skyline. At its left end rises the wide hump of the Cheviot (815 m).

- Slant slightly right down the open field, passing through the storm-damaged clump of trees to reach a further gate onto a grassy track at mile 28·8. Turn right downhill, and within 500 m turn sharp left along a minor road beside Bowmont Water.
- After nearly a mile of road, pass Primsidemill on the right, go over the minor crossroads and rise to meet the B6401, where you turn right towards Yetholm.
- After 650 m of the B6401 reach a cemetery and at its far end turn right into a minor road. Within 80 m turn left on a green track towards Bowmont Water.
- Follow the track for 0·7 miles (1·1 km) as it heads north and crosses a field, becoming a barely trod path. Just maintain direction but veer left near the road to find the gate just left of an electricity substation. Exit to the road bridge between the two Yetholms. At mile 31·2 this marks the half-way point of the Way.
- If staying in Town Yetholm, turn left at the road bridge, otherwise turn right to cross the Bowmont Water.
- On its far side, the Way descends steps to a path that continues beside the river. It crosses a field, then bends right into the streets of Kirk Yetholm. For the famous Border Hotel (terminus of the Pennine Way) aim for the eastern side of The Green.

THIS MEMORIAL REMINDS US OF THE GYPSY TRIBE WHO INHABITED THIS VILLAGE FROM THE 17th CENTURY ONWARDS. THEIR CUSTOMS AND TRADITIONS INFLUENCED MANY ASPECTS OF VILLAGE LIFE. THE LATE VIC TOKELY WHO RESEARCHED AND RELATED THEIR HISTORY THROUGHOUT THE BORDERS INSPIRED THIS PERMANENT REMINDER OF THEIR LEGACY
2003

Kirk Yetholm Gypsies

A law of 1609 made it legal in Scotland to kill Gypsies. Many of the Gypsies retreated to the edge of the hills, where they could find refuge in times of persecution. They are recorded in Kirk Yetholm as early as 1695, including the Gypsy royal family, surnamed Faa. Jean Gordon Faa, the first Gypsy Queen in Kirk Yetholm, inspired the character Meg Merilies in Sir Walter Scott's 1815 novel Guy Mannering. In real life she was banned from Kirk Yetholm for fighting with another woman, and finally was put to death by drowning for supporting the Jacobite Rising. You pass the Gypsy Palace, now a small holiday cottage, on the Way out of Kirk Yetholm.

Clump of trees on the descent from Crookedshaws

3.3 Kirk Yetholm to Wooler

Distance	13·3 miles (21·6 km)
Terrain	moorland paths and tracks, with one indistinct section (leaving Hethpool) and one boggy section (after Yeavering Bell)
Grade	first half has steep climb out of Kirk Yetholm across the border at 340 m (1115 ft), then descent to Hethpool; second half climbs to undulating section on high moorland followed by descent to Wooler
Food and drink	Wooler (shops, café, hotels)
Summary	the Way's toughest section, mostly across high moorlands, rewarded by fine views northwards, especially from the track over Gains Law

49 51 55 57

31·5 — 1·9 — 3·2 — 4·7 — 3·5 — 44·8
Kirk Yetholm 3·1 Border 5·1 Hethpool 7·6 Gains Law 5·6 Wooler

- At The Green, find the fingerpost, information boards and gypsy memorial clustered in the grass near the Border Hotel. From here, for its first 2 miles (3 km) St Cuthbert's Way shares the route with Pennine Way so you will see its signage too, often with an acorn logo.

- Follow the fingerpost up the lane signed Halterburn Penial Revival Centre. It climbs steeply, then descends to Halter Burn glen.

- At the valley floor, a fingerpost points uphill for both Pennine and St Cuthbert's Ways.

- After a cattle grid bear left along the fence to cross the burn by a foot-bridge. Cross the small ravine of the Shielknowe Burn to a stone wall and head uphill on a green path, at first with the wall to your left.

- At the wall's corner, bear right uphill, to contour around Green Humbleton hill.

- Keep ahead as a smaller path crosses diagonally. The main path heads uphill on the spur above Green Humbleton, to a fingerpost announcing that the Pennine and St Cuthbert's Ways diverge here, at mile 33·2.

South-west over the Border ridge

- Turn left beside the burn as signed by the fingerpost 'Elsdonburn 1½'. The path rises slightly towards a gate through the border fence and wall. The fingerpost carries a message 'Welcome to Scotland/Welcome to England'.
- The grass path continues across the border ridge. Prominent to your left is Eccles Cairn, worth a 5-minute detour for finer views. The easiest access is by a trod path that turns off left just before a waymarker, and before you start to descend.
- The route now descends quite steeply into the valley of Elsdon Burn, with lovely open views ahead. The descent is boggy in places but generally runs slightly north of east.
- The path crosses a stream and enters the fenced area of a felled plantation by a curious gate-stile which may oblige you to remove a large rucksack before you can wriggle through.
- Within 500 m, emerge from the fenced area by a matching gate-stile and descend across an open field. Cross this slightly downhill to pick up a farm track at mile 34·6.
- The track passes through gates, fords a stream, rises briefly, then drops to Elsdonburn Farm. Wind your way down past the buildings in front of the house to the start of a tarmac lane.
- The lane snakes down the valley: ignore any turnoffs and at mile 36·4 join a minor road at its corner. Turn right to reach Hethpool within 300 m.

Descent toward Elsdon Burn

Below Yeavering Bell

- After the entrance to Hethpool House the road bends right, but the Way leaves it by turning left to cross a bridge over College Burn at mile 36·7. At once turn left up a rougher track that rises gently and then runs through a plantation to a gate.

- A rough path continues across the hillside, boggy in places. Reach a gateway and turn left into an area of tall gorse bushes, followed by an area colonised mainly by birch trees.

- After a few metres, turn right onto a path that dips to cross a stream by stepping stones. The path then rises to emerge from the gorse at a stile.

- Now a path slants left, gently uphill and slightly north of east, to pass above a stone sheep pen – possible shelter for a picnic stop.

- Follow a rough track that starts here, running gently uphill and through a spruce plantation. Bypass Torleehouse by taking a narrow path on the right just above the track, rejoining the track beyond the house. Follow the broad track downhill for 400 m. Just before a cattle grid, turn off right on a grassy track at mile 38·2.

Torleehouse

- After 100 m the track goes left through a gate. It appproaches a triangular patch of woodland at mile 38·4, but bends uphill to the right before reaching it. The track heads up a grassy spur, by way of a gate with ladder stile on the left.
- Cross onto a wide grassy path that runs uphill, slanting along the steep side of a valley. Opposite is the hill fort of Yeavering Bell, with a necklace of fallen stonework around its summit.
- Ignore a path that forks left down to a timber post, it's not SCW. Instead keep ahead soon passing ground-level timber signs at a path crossroads. The two SCW discs clearly confirm the Way is straight on.
- About 800 m after the crossroads, the gradient levels off at about mile 39·3. Look for where you fork left on a smaller path with waymarker post.
- Ahead, and distant to the left, you'll see the stony outcrop of Tom Tallon's Crag on the horizon. The Way takes you closer to the crag but stays well below it.

Continue across the path crossroads

- At a path junction, bear right along a narrow path through the heather to a gate/stile. Descend to the corner of a broad track. Follow it ahead, down to and through a gate.
- The track bends right across the Akeld Burn by footbridge at mile 39·9. At once turn off left on a grass path that soon becomes peaty and boggy.
- The path heads south-east past a conical cairn, then gently uphill. Aim towards the gateway in a skyline wall, until (just before it) you turn left up a wide track.

Looking back to Tom Tallon's Crag

Distant view of the North Sea ahead

- The track follows the wall and then passes through it at a gate to join a wider track. For the next 2·5 miles/4 km, this track gives easy moorland walking, and perhaps your first views of the sea ahead.

- Follow the track north-east along a long moorland hump with the wall on your left at first.

- At mile 41, the track leaves the wall and bends right to cross the head of a steep valley. Now it veers further right to pass around the shoulder of Gains Law. Ahead to the left is Humbleton Hill with its hill fort: see panel.

- Stay on the track as it bends left to go through a gate where heathery ground gives way to grassland. The track bends slightly right and descends gradually around the northern flank of Coldberry Hill.

- The Way bends left and descends more steeply to go through a gateway. At once, turn right off the broad grassy track. Another gate leads to a grassy path running east.

Humbleton Hill

Humbleton Hill has an Iron Age hill fort. If you divert over it, you can drop down to Humbleton village for a short-cut into Wooler. The hill was the site of a battle in 1402 between two great Border families: the Percies of Northumberland and the Douglases of Scotland. The Scots' defeat was recorded by Shakespeare, who refers to the battle as Holmedon (Henry IV Part 1).

A steep grassy hollow separates Humbleton Hill from the moorland crossed by the Way. This 'meltwater channel' is the course carved by a small river in the Ice Age, when its natural run-off to the north was blocked by ice.

North-east over Wooler

- After 300 m the path bends right, to a gate at the top of a plantation. An earth path leads down through it and across a footbridge to the car park at Wooler Common (mile 42·9). The Way turns right here.
- The road to the left, Common Road, is a short-cut into Wooler that misses out some fairly impressive earthworks, but if saving 800 m (and about 100 m of height gain) is important you could take it. If so, skip the next four bullets on page 56 and rejoin the Way at mile 44·3.
- Out of the car park turn right, at once forking left at a signpost just before a stream. A path leads upstream, with forest on its left, for 300 m.

- At the wood corner the path turns uphill through gorse. You are aiming for the top corner of the same plantation but the direct path is not a right-of-way, so fork right to meet a fence.
- Turn sharp left and descend beside the fence to a gate at the plantation corner. The path now runs uphill, with trees on its left at first, then on both sides, to a clearing.
- Follow the path ahead along the clearing, then downhill through the trees to a gate out of the plantation. The grassy path continues ahead, with the Kettles earthworks on its right, near mile 44.
- The path wanders downhill into a reed-filled valley, where it bends left to the driveway of Waud Hause. The track leads down to join Common Road at mile 44·3, at the edge of Wooler.
- Turn right down Common Road, which descends to become Ramsey's Lane. (At the name change, a signed bridleway path on the right offers a shortcut to Wooler Youth Hostel and Shepherds Huts.)
- Otherwise the street leads down into Wooler's Market Place. Turn left here for the High Street and many of Wooler's facilities including the Tourist Information Centre in Padgepool Place, or turn right for Cheviot Street and another route to the Youth Hostel. From Market Place, the Way continues diagonally opposite, heading down Church Street.

St Mary's Church, Wooler

War memorial and castle masonry on Tower Hill, Wooler

Wooler

Wooler's name probably means 'well on the hill', and it has been settled since the Stone Age. The Kettles, the Iron Age settlement just above the town, was reused by the Romans, and many cup-and-ring marked rocks are to the east. Wooler's first recorded mention was in 1107: 'situated in an ill-cultivated country under the influence of vast mountains ... subject to impetuous rains'. It has been a busy market town since its charter was granted in 1199.

Lying so close both to the hills and to the border, it suffered severely in the reiving times, being attacked by Scots in both 1340 and 1409. The town was garrisoned at various times by both nations. It had a fortified tower dating from c.1550, which replaced a 12th-century wooden castle. Parts of the tower are still visible: the photo on page 56 shows an impressive part of its masonry on Tower Hill, just south-east of St Mary's Church.

Street names such as Tenter Hill underline the importance of Wooler's weaving trade. 'Tenters' are frames on which the woven cloth is stretched out after weaving. Wooler's large number of inns suggest its former importance on the turnpike road to Scotland, now bypassed by the A1. Its community website is at *www.wooler.org.uk*.

3·4 Wooler to Fenwick

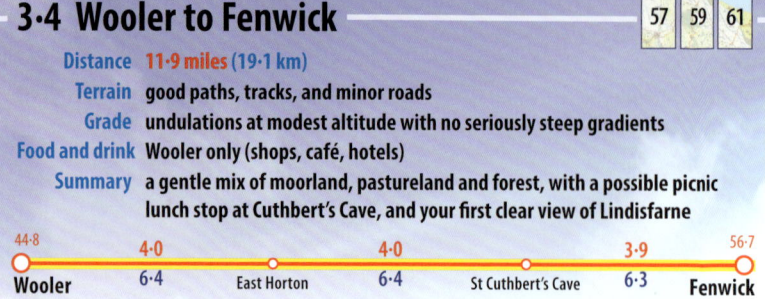

Distance	**11·9 miles (19·1 km)**
Terrain	good paths, tracks, and minor roads
Grade	undulations at modest altitude with no seriously steep gradients
Food and drink	Wooler only (shops, café, hotels)
Summary	a gentle mix of moorland, pastureland and forest, with a possible picnic lunch stop at Cuthbert's Cave, and your first clear view of Lindisfarne

```
44·8      4·0              4·0                3·9       56·7
Wooler  6·4  East Horton  6·4  St Cuthbert's Cave  6·3  Fenwick
```

- From Wooler's Market Place, go past St Mary's Church on the right and head down Church Street. Within 300 m cross the A697 making a right-left dogleg into Weetwood Road (B6348).
- Cross the Wooler Water by a steel-arch road bridge and within 40 m turn right past the bowling green on a lane. This briefly becomes a footpath along the backs of houses, then a road again (Weetwood Avenue).
- At its end, turn left to go uphill on Brewery Road, past the school and recycling centre. After 900 m, the road bends decisively right. Instead, at mile 45·7 take a path (later bridleway) on the left, steeply up to the top of Weetwood Moor. (Across the moorland to the right of the Way is a cup-and-ring marked rock: see the panel and photo on page 59.)
- The pleasant, grassy path runs around the moorland rim. Pass the remnants of stone farm buildings, then go along the right edge of a plantation towards another one.
- Approach the near corner of the second plantation (mile 46·9) and turn left through a gate before it. Head diagonally to a kissing-gate at the corner of another plantation, then turn downhill to the left.

Descent toward Weetwood Bridge

Cup and ring marked rock

Cup-and-ring marks probably date from the late Stone Age. Nobody knows their meaning or function. The sandstone of Weetwood Moor has several, one only 250 m from the Way – though it takes careful searching (or a GPS).

As the Way levels out around mile 46.2, there's a waymarked path junction. From this point head south past two boulders at the moor top. Once the nearby radio mast lies directly south-west, start looking for a flat-topped rock. Alternatively, if you have a GPS, set it to NU 01020 28020.

As several thousand years of wind and rain have been eroding the markings, they are best seen under the low sun of morning or evening.

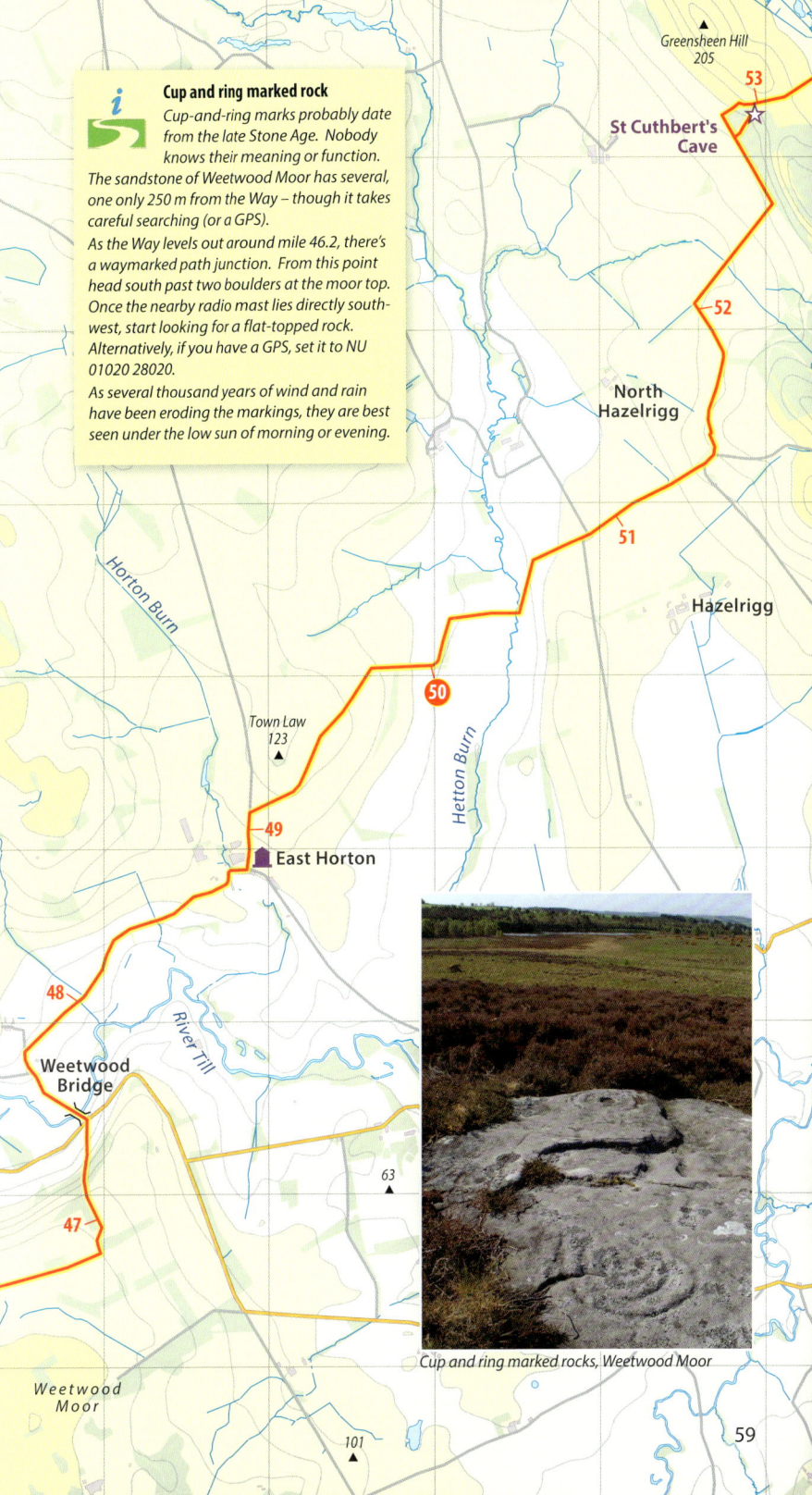

Cup and ring marked rocks, Weetwood Moor

59

- The path bends down to a small gate marked only with a Public Footpath yellow arrow. Go through on a narrow path that winds down among trees. Cross the field below to a ladder stile to the road to Weetwood Bridge.
- Cross this bridge over the River Till. Within 400 m the lane bends right for 'Hortons, Lowick'. Follow the lane for a further 1·1 miles (1·8 km) to East Horton Farmhouse (B&B). Turn left, signed for 'Lowick, Ancroft'.

- After 300 m turn right off the Devil's Causeway on a lane, on tarmac at first. After it starts to descend, pass a well-preserved World War 2 pillbox on the right, now on a looser surface. At the bottom, keep left on the main track, which crosses Hetton Burn at mile 50·4.
- Turn left and follow the track as it climbs to a road junction with a house on the right. Go straight ahead into the lane signed for Belford. After 800 m, ignore a road on the right, but 80 m later turn left on a green track at mile 51·5.
- After 120 m go through a gate on the right. Follow the path along the foot of the field, and descend to go through a gate.
- Continue across the next field with a hedge to the left, down to a staggered junction at mile 52. Here turn sharp right up a track that starts gravelly then turns grassy, to the foot of the wooded steeper slope above.
- Go through the gate and turn left along the plantation foot, continuing just inside it. A path at mile 52·8 runs up right towards St Cuthbert's Cave: see the panel on page 61. If you follow this to the cave, you need not backtrack downhill; instead cross rough ground to a timber stile above the cave to its left.
- However, the Way bypasses the cave, keeping ahead along the plantation edge to its bottom corner. Just outside, it turns sharp right, uphill to the top corner of the pine wood, where damage from Storm Arwen was still evident in 2023.
- At the ridgeline, turn left through a gate, and at once left again through a lesser gate. You may enjoy your first clear views of the North Sea ahead. A short detour up to the left here gains Greensheen Hill. It's a good spot for picnics, rocky scrambles, and even for geology.

St Cuthbert's Cave

St Cuthbert's Cave

The cave is a natural one, eroded out of yellow Fell Sandstone, standing in a mature pine wood. It has room to shelter several people.

Escaping the Danish raid of AD875, Bishop Eardulf of Lindisfarne and the monks carried St Cuthbert's body around Britain for seven years. According to legend, this cave was one of their first stops. The body then visited Cumberland, south-west Scotland, Ripon in Yorkshire and even Melrose, Cuthbert's early home. When it was placed on a ship at Whitehaven, with the intention of carrying it across to Ireland, a rain of blood from the sky indicated that the saint should not be removed. His body eventually found a safe resting place at Durham.

- From the two gates the path heads downhill, gradually diverging from a fence on the right to cross a footbridge. Cross the next field on the same heading to a gate. From here, enjoy your first clear view of Lindisfarne and its castle ahead.
- Bend left to and through another signposted gate, onto a track. Turn left, signed for Holburn. The track bends to the right with a fence, and passes a small pond.
- Enter the plantation and within a few metres turn right (mile 54·2) on a forest road that soon bends left to run generally northwards. Ignore a fingerpost pointing right to Detchant Park and stick to the main track as it descends.

- After about 600 m, just after a small cleared area with open views, the track bends right, but a fingerpost at mile 54·6 turns you off left onto a narrow path, still heading north. It promises 'Fenwick 2' and it's downhill all the way.
- In 2023 the path was muddy and obstructed in places by damage from Storm Arwen and forestry work. It descends to pass straight over another forest track, but in places the route is indistinct and deflected by the odd fallen tree. Orange paint splashes help to point the route.
- Finally cross two footbridges, a stile and a third footbridge before emerging to a field corner by a step-stile.
- The Way continues downhill for a further mile, with the wood on its left and fields on the right.
- Near the bottom, the path runs with a hedge on its left, turns left through a gateway, then runs with another hedge on its right to emerge at a lane, opposite a house (Blawearie).

The Way approaching Blawearie and the lane

- Turn right for 800 m, and follow the lane down to pass the Village Hall (where the Guru coffee shop is worth a visit if open) to a T-junction in Fenwick at mile 56·7.
- To continue the Way, or to reach the A1 for buses from Fenwick Bridge, turn right and skip to page 63.

  Unless you have found somewhere to stay in Fenwick you will probably be overnighting at the Lindisfarne Inn, handy for catching a tidal window to cross the causeway.
- In that case, instead turn left at the mile 56·7 T-junction and within 300 m bear right along the lane (Cycle route 1). After a further 1·4 miles (2·3 km) this leads to the A1 at Beal. Arriva buses X15 and X18 stop on the both sides of the A1. To reach the Lindisfarne Inn and filling station with shop, cross the busy trunk road with great care.
- From Beal, continue on the road to pass the Barn at Beal (restaurant and campsite) within one mile. The start of the Lindisfarne causeway is just 0·9 miles (1·4 km) beyond. Skip to page 66.

The Lindisfarne Inn

3.5 Fenwick to Lindisfarne

Distance 5·9 miles (9·5 km)
Terrain field paths and causeway (or tidal mud on Pilgrims Way)
Grade after a gentle rise over Fenhamhill, the remaining route is at or below sea level
Food and drink none until Holy Island village (shop, hotels, cafés)
Summary a short field section leads to the unforgettable crossing of Beal Sands to the Holy Island of Lindisfarne

Fenwick 56·7 — 2·3 — 3·7 — Causeway — 3·6 — 5·8 — Lindisfarne 62·6

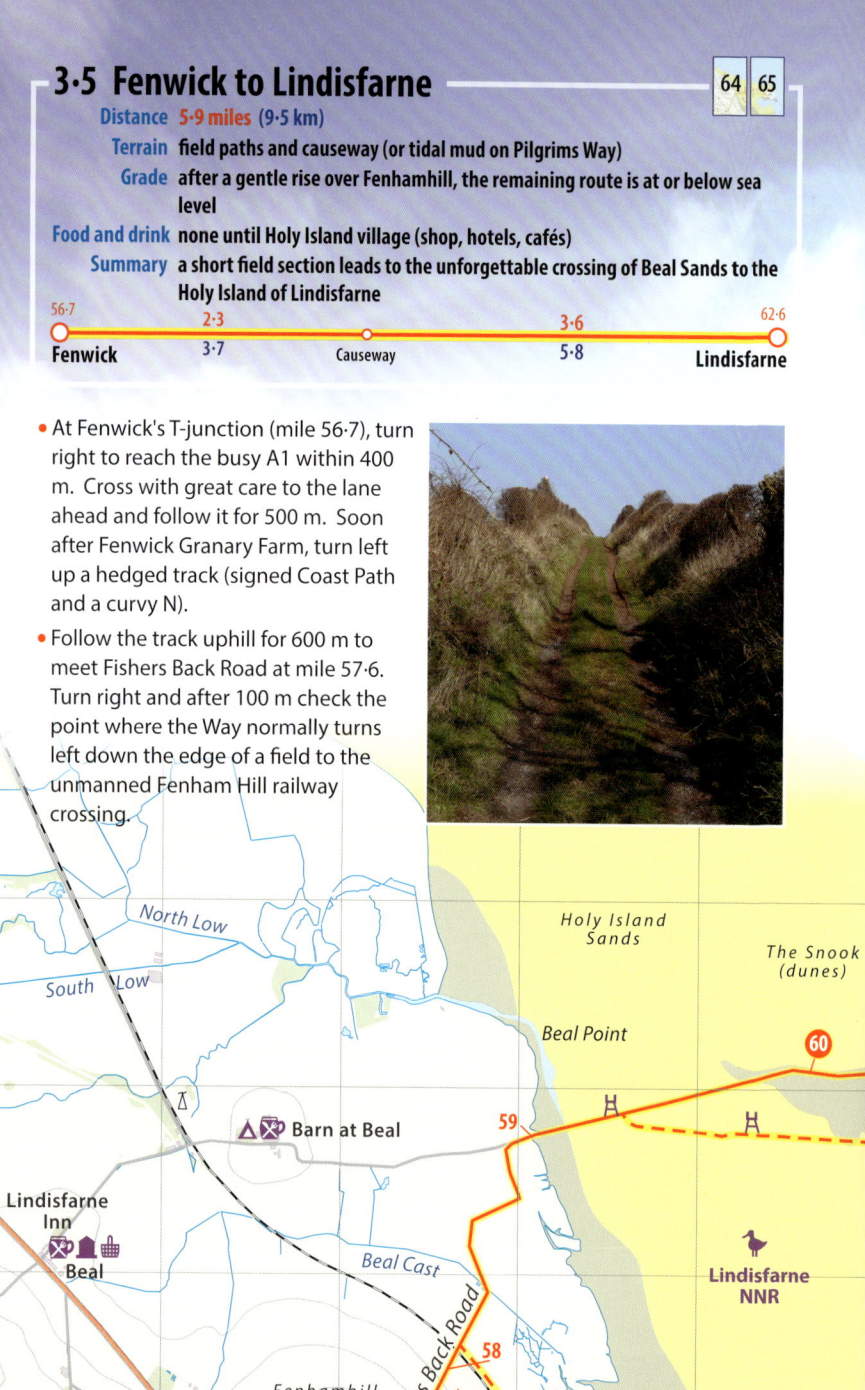

- At Fenwick's T-junction (mile 56·7), turn right to reach the busy A1 within 400 m. Cross with great care to the lane ahead and follow it for 500 m. Soon after Fenwick Granary Farm, turn left up a hedged track (signed Coast Path and a curvy N).

- Follow the track uphill for 600 m to meet Fishers Back Road at mile 57·6. Turn right and after 100 m check the point where the Way normally turns left down the edge of a field to the unmanned Fenham Hill railway crossing.

- The unmanned crossing was temporarily closed by Network Rail during 2023 for safety improvements, but once reopened is the preferred route. *Always* use the yellow phone to speak with the signalman before crossing in case a high-speed train is approaching. Failure to use the phone is not only dangerous, but also it increases the chances that Network Rail may try to make the closure permanent.
- When it's safe, cross the lines with care and go straight onto a path heading north-east: skip the next bullet to continue the Way.
- If the unmanned crossing is closed, or if walking in a group makes it seem advisable, instead keep ahead on Fishers Back Road which crosses over the railway after 800 m. Drop down to follow the path beside the railway northward. After a further 800 m, at the unmanned crossing turn right: this detour is shown on map page 64 and is well signed when in force.
- The path goes over a footbridge above a drainage ditch. Fork left to cross a field diagonally to a gate at its far corner. Signage in this final section may also show Coast Path (with a curvy N), St Oswald's Way (with a raven logo), an acorn or (most recent) England Coast Path – or any combination.
- Bear right on a track, and after 150 m bear right again on a grass path across a field to reach the shoreline with its avenue of anti-tank blocks dating from World War 2. If you've arrived near low tide, you may struggle to see any sea beyond the mud flats.

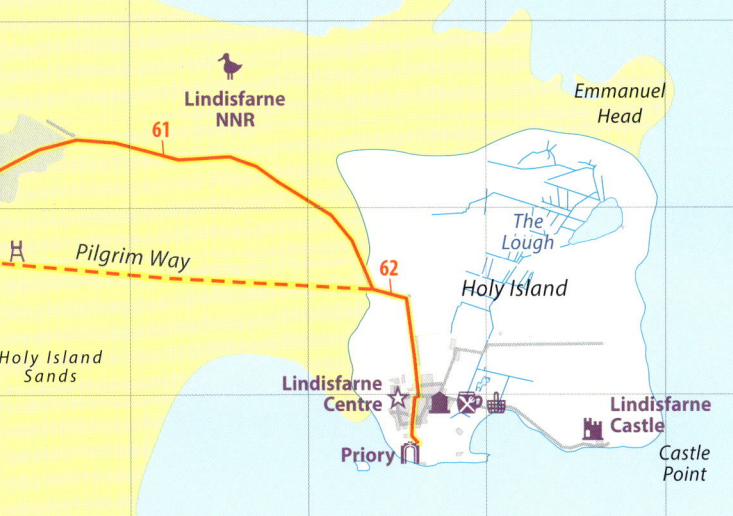

- Turn left between the rows of anti-tank blocks, to reach the road at the end of the Lindisfarne causeway. Check the safe crossing times shown on the board here before proceeding.
- Turn right along the causeway across the mudflats to the refuge on stilts where the causeway crosses a permanent river.
- If it is safe, here you can turn off the busy road to the Pilgrim Way across the sand and mud. Read the last two paragraphs of page 11 before deciding whether time and tide permit.
- Otherwise keep to the road along the causeway to the sand dunes of Lindisfarne. Walk around its bay to pass the large car park at the north edge of Holy Island village.
- Follow the road into the village to a T-junction where the priory is ahead. This is the official end of the Way: congratulations!

 Pilgrim Way
More adventurous and romantic, from the bridge and refuge shelter, is to follow tall poles that mark the Pilgrim Way across the sands. For 1500 years until the building of the road causeway, this was the only route to Holy Island. The marker poles and refuge shelters were raised in the 1990s. Bare feet are best. Most of the going is firm but there will be usually be some short sections of oozy mud, as well as shallow pools and streams to wade through. The Pilgrim Way rejoins the road just north of Holy Island village.

Causeway with refuge, dawn

Lindisfarne

Lindisfarne Priory

Lindisfarne is the Saxon name: *farne* means 'retreat', but probably a retreat from dangerous enemies rather than a religious one. Since the time of Cuthbert, it has been known as Holy Island. Today its formal title is 'the Holy Island of Lindisfarne'.

The island's resident population is less than 200. Today it is a place of pilgrimage not only for Christians, but also for naturalists, bird-watchers and archaeologists. Over 500,000 people visit each year, and 50,000 birds over-winter here.

Cuthbert's priory is now a roofless ruin, with stone columns reaching upwards towards the sky. North Sea breezes blowing through the high arches have furrowed the soft sandstone, the wind erosion obvious after just a few short centuries.

A statue of St Aidan, the priory's founder, stands outside the entrance. Behind it is a tall cross that could be considered the final waymark of St Cuthbert's Way. There's an entry fee for the priory itself, but the surrounding graveyard is accessible at any time. At its end, next to the shore, is a modern statue of St Cuthbert.

Nearby in Holy Island village is the Lindisfarne Centre. Here is a beautiful replica of the Lindisfarne Gospels, the original being held at the British Library. There is a display on the Viking raid of AD793, and an introduction to the wildlife and ecology of the island.

As you head out of the village to the harbour, you come across a line of old fishing boats, inverted and painted with pitch for waterproofing. These are used as stores by the Lindisfarne fishermen. The harbour itself is tidal, with bare mud at low water. It is used mainly by pleasure yachts.

Beyond rises Lindisfarne Castle. It was built in 1550, using stones looted from the Priory ruins, to guard the harbour. Early in the 20th century it was converted to a family home by the architect Edwin Lutyens (designer of New Delhi and of the Cenotaph in London). He used the natural textures of stone, slate and timber to atmospheric effect. To the north of the castle is the walled garden created for it by the famous designer Gertrude Jekyll. It has recently been restored to its original planting scheme.

East of the castle are handsome Victorian limekilns. The island's limestone was processed here before being carried away by boat for use in the fields and in making mortar for building. Onwards to the north lie the 10 km of sand dunes and salt marsh and tidal mud, the island's unique wildlife zone. The rare plants, seals and tens of thousands of birds have been described briefly in Section 2.3. To study them in full could take a lifetime.

After four, five, or six days of walking, Lindisfarne is a place to stand still – to gaze across the North Sea at sunrise, to watch the sea mist threading through the high arch of the Priory, to see the tide creep inwards and the seabirds move up towards you across the mud.

Lindisfarne opening times
Lindisfarne attractions are mostly open only in season (in 2023 mid-March to October). The castle opening times vary with the causeway crossing times and it's best to book a time slot (closed on Fridays). The Lindisfarne Centre opens daily in season 10.00 to 16.30, tides permitting. The Priory is also open daily in season, tides permitting, but weekends only out of season. See page 70 for links to their websites.

Lindisfarne Castle from the village

Rucksack Readers

Award-winning guidebooks to long-distance walks, mainly in the UK and Ireland but with a selection of adventurous walks worldwide.

Visit our website for a list of titles, sample pages and images from the books; with route resources such as mapping that is zoomable to extreme detail, useful links and GPX files: **www.rucsacs.com**

All Rucksack Readers guidebooks are written by walkers for walkers, with options where appropriate for cyclists. The books are lavishly illustrated with custom mapping and 70-120 colour photos. They are rugged, lightweight and on rainproof paper.

www.rucsacs.com / info@rucsacs.com

Five selected pilgrimage routes

Below are five pilgrimage routes, all of which can be completed in about one week and provide opportunities for reflection and renewal for people of any religion or none: bring your own beliefs. Immerse yourself in the natural world while also learning more about some remarkable historic figures, saints and radical thinkers.

There are Rucksack Readers guidebooks on the five routes below: see *www.rucsacs.com*.

For comprehensive data on pilgrimage routes in Britain visit the British Pilgrimage Trust website: *www.britishpilgrimage.org*.

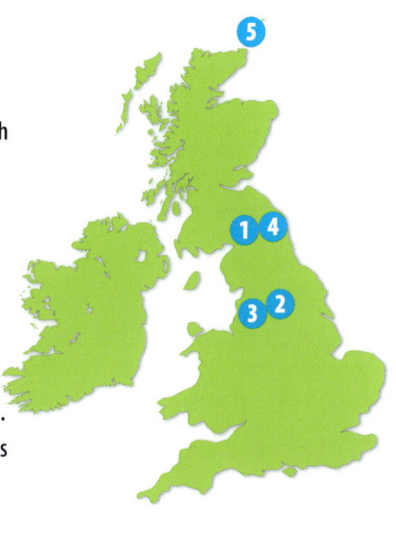

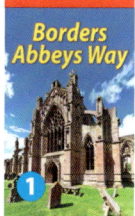

1 Circuit from Melrose
67 miles 108 km

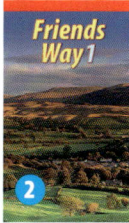

2 Barley to Sedbergh
62 miles 100 km

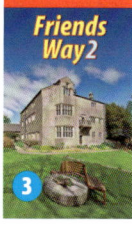

3 Sedbergh to Swarthmoor
58 miles 94 km

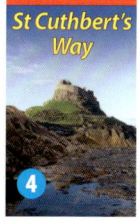

4 Melrose to Lindisfarne
62 miles 100 km

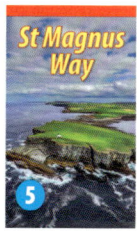

5 Gurness to Kirkwall
60 miles 96 km

4 Reference

Useful websites
The official website for this route is
   www.stcuthbertsway.info
For lots of information visit our web page
   rucsacs.com/books/scw
For a list of other useful links, visit our page
   bit.ly/RR-scw-links

Ranger service
Three authorities maintain and manage the Way. Contact the relevant one to report problems with access/waymarking or to appreciate their work:

Melrose to English Border: Scottish Borders Council Ranger Service
   01835 825 070
   rangers@scotborders.gov.uk

English Border to Wooler Common: Northumberland National Park Ranger Service (North)
   01669 620 414
   ranger@nnpa.org.uk

Wooler to Lindisfarne: Northumberland County Council's Countryside Section
   0345 600 6400
   countryside@northumberland.gov.uk

Weather and tides
Weather forecasts are available online and via local radio/TV.

The Met Office is Britain's authoritative source of accurate forecasts
   www.metoffice.gov.uk
For use on mobile devices, obtain its Weather Forecast app.

Lindisfarne causeway safe crossing times:
   bit.ly/RR-causeway
   or call 01289 330 733 (Berwick TIC) for tide times, which are also posted on the door at Wooler TIC and at the mainland end of the causeway.

Maps (printed and online) and GPX
Harvey Maps publishes a waterproof 1:40,000 strip map of the whole route:
   www.harveymaps.co.uk. Other UK maps, including Explorer sheets 338, 340 and OL16 are available from
   www.ordnancesurvey.co.uk

For an accurate route map that you can zoom repeatedly for incredible detail, visit
   rucsacs.com/books/scw
and click the map graphic. The same page offers a GPX file for free download.

Access
Everyone has the right to be on most land and inland water in Scotland providing they act responsibly: see
   www.outdooraccess-scotland.com
from which you can download the *Scottish Outdoor Access Code* and *Dog Owners* leaflet.

The whole of the Way in England runs on rights of way, and much of the upland ground alongside it is open access land, marked by a '*brown walker*' waymark. Visit *www.naturalengland.org.uk* and search for open access land.

Places of Interest
For Borders abbeys visit
   www.historicenvironment.scot
and search for Melrose, Dryburgh and Jedburgh. In 2023 there were some access restrictions while masonry inspections took place. Normal opening hours are 10.00-17.00 in season with earlier closing out of season.

Mary Queen of Scots' House, Jedburgh
   bit.ly/RR-mqs   tel 01835 863 331
Three Hills Roman Heritage Centre, Melrose
   www.trimontium.co.uk
Monteviot House
   www.monteviot.com

Lindisfarne Castle is managed by the National Trust and its page is here:
   bit.ly/RR-lind-castle
Lindisfarne Priory
   www.english-heritage.org.uk
Lindisfarne National Nature Reserve
   www.naturalengland.org.uk
The Lindisfarne Centre
   www.lindisfarnecentre.org

Visitor information sources
On the Scottish side, the only iCentre near the route is at Jedburgh, next to the bus station (Murray's Green) tel 01835 863 170 or email
   jedburgh@visitscotland.com

On the English side, tourist information is available from the Cheviot Centre, Wooler NE71 6BL, open Mon-Fri 10.00-14.00 (longer hours in season): tel 01668 282 123 or email
   wooler.tic@northumberland.gov.uk

Berwick-upon-Tweed also has a TIC open daily year-round but closed on Sundays
   01289 330 733
The Library Building, Walkergate, Berwick-upon-Tweed TD15 1DB.

Support services
Several companies provide complete packages (including accommodation booking) and one specialises in baggage transfer for the route: visit our website for an updated list:
   bit.ly/scw-support

Taxi firms
You need to book ahead for rural taxis, and ideally choose a firm whose location is close to where the lift is needed. Five Star Taxis cover Melrose, Jedburgh and beyond; Hownam Taxis are based in Kelso but cover a wide area and Glendale Taxis are based in Wooler.

Five Star Taxis	01896 756 789
Hownam Taxis	01573 440 389
Glendale Taxis	01668 282 292

Transport
For travel from anywhere to anywhere, try
   rome2rio.com
Traveline covers public transport throughout the UK:
   traveline.info
For trains between Edinburgh and Tweedbank:
   scotrail.co.uk
For Borders Buses (see pages 9-10)
   bordersbuses.co.uk
For journey planning and bus timetables in Northumberland
   arrivabus.co.uk/north-east
For travel to/from Lindisfarne:
   www.lindisfarne.org.uk
National Express:
   www.nationalexpress.com
Newcastle Airport
   www.newcastleairport.com
Edinburgh Airport
   www.edinburghairport.com

Hostels
There are two hostels on the Way, one at Kirk Yetholm (TD5 8PG)
   friendsofnature.org.uk/houses/kirk-yetholm
   01573 420 639
and the other is the Youth Hostel and Shepherds' Huts at Wooler (NE71 6LW)
   www.woolerhostel.co.uk
   01668 281 365

Pilgrimage links
The British Pilgrimage Trust is a charity that helps to develop and promote a network of hundreds of pilgrimage routes including this one:
   www.britishpilgrimage.org
Northern Cross runs an annual Christian group pilgrimage in Easter week
   www.northerncross.co.uk

Notes for novices
For advice on preparation, distance planning and equipment, scroll to the foot of our home page and click the yellow button:
   www.rucsacs.com

Acknowledgements
We thank the ranger services for their work in maintaining the Way, and Roger Smith, Ron Shaw and Scottish Borders Council who devised and developed it. We thank the following for commenting on drafts: Phil Bradley (Countryside Section, Northumberland County Council), Lorna Lazzari (Northumberland National Park Authority), Ben McCallum (Scottish Borders Council Ranger Service) and Neil Rawlins (LDWA). The author thanks David Howard for company along the original walk. The publisher thanks Lindsay Merriman for painstaking proofreading.

Photo credits
We thank the following for their images: *Dreamstime.com* with Julianelliott title page, with Ivan Kravtsov p21 and with Elena Duvernay p23l; Durham Cathedral p19; *geograph.org.uk* with Jim Barton 20l, with Barbara Carr p56l and with Rob Gray p15l; *istockphoto.com* with Alistair Scott p18, with Herbert Kratky p25 mid and with topshotUK p27u; Lindisfarne Inn p63l; Jacquetta Megarry p12 (all 7), p13 (all 6), p14, p27l, p29, p32 (mid), p35, p36, p38u, p40, p41u, p44l, p45l, p46u, p48u, p50 (all 3), p52 (lower 2), p53 (both), p54u, p56u, p60u, p62 (both), p63u, p64, p65, p66u; Sandy Morrison p23u; Gordon Simm p26 inset; St Cuthbert Centre, Lindisfarne pp10-11; untraceable source p5; *wayfaringkiwi.com* p45u; all 41 other photos including front and back covers by Ronald Turnbull.

Index

A
access 14, 70
accommodation and supplies 8–9
altitude profile 12-13

B
Beal 7, 8, 9, 10, 63,
Borders Abbeys Way 13, 32, 33, 36, 39
Bowden 32
bus travel 9–10, 71
buzzard 23

C
camping 7, 8
causeway 'safe period' 6, 10, 11, 63, 66, 70
Cessford Castle 21, 40, 43, 44
coastal habitat 5, 27
Common Ridings 15, 21, 38
Crystal Well 34
cup-and-ring marked rocks 57, 58, 59

D
Dere Street 5, 20, 35, 39, 41
distances and time needed 6–7
dogs 14
Dryburgh Abbey 7, 20, 21, 33, 70

E
eider (Cuddy) duck 27
Eildon Hills 4, 17, 20, 22, 31, 33, 44
emergency, tidal 11

F
Fenwick 7, 8, 63, 64

G
Gains Law 26, 54
Galashiels 9
geology 22, 25, 27, 41
goosander 23
grouse, red 26

H
habitats and wildlife 22–27
hare, brown 25
Harestanes 7, 8, 36, 39, 40
heather 20, 22, 26
heron, grey 24
Hethpool 8, 50, 52
history and heritage 20–21, 57, 61
hostels 8, 56, 71
Humbleton Hill 54

J
Jedburgh 7, 8, 10, 15, 20, 21, 36, 38, 41, 70

L
Lilliard 21, 35
Lindisfarne (Holy Island of) 4–6, 7, 9, 10, 11, 12, 66-68, 70
Lindisfarne (Priory) 17–19, 67, 70

M
maps, mapping 13, 70
Melrose 5, 7–9, 10, 15, 17, 18, 20, 24, 28, 30-1, 70

midges 5, 16
mobile phones (cellphones) 16
Morebattle 5, 6, 8, 9, 44

N
Newtown St Boswells 7, 32

O
oystercatcher 27

P
packing checklist 16
Pennine Way 13, 46, 48,
Pilgrim Way 4, 5, 6, 11, 12, 16, 27, 66
planning your walk 5–14

S
salmon 23-4
Scottish Outdoor Access Code 14, 70
St Boswells 6, 7, 8, 24, 33, 34
Synod of Whitby 17, 18

T
tides, tidal danger 6, 7, 10–11, 17, 66, 68, 70
transport, public 8-9, 71
Tweed, River 5, 7, 23–24, 34

V
visitor information 70

W
Waterloo Monument 39, 45
waymarking 13
weather 5–6, 70
Wideopen Hill 5, 16, 45
wildlife 4, 14, 22–27
Wooler 15, 54, 55, 56, 57, 58, 70

Y
Yeavering Bell 20, 52-3
Yetholms (Town and Kirk) 7, 8, 9, 45, 46, 48, 71
yellowhammer 25